CONFEDERATION IN CRISIS

EDITED BY ROBERT YOUNG

CONFEDERATION IN CRISIS

EDITED BY ROBERT YOUNG

James Lorimer & Company, Publishers
Toronto, 1991

Canadian Cataloguing in Publication Data

Main entry under title:

Confederation in crisis

Proceedings of a symposium held at the University of
Western Ontario on Nov. 9, 1990.
Includes bibliographical references.
ISBN 1-55028-327-8 (bound) ISBN 1-55028-325-1 (pbk.)

1. Canada — Constitutional law — Amendments —
Congresses. 2. Federal government — Canada —
Congresses. I. Young, Robert Andrew.
II. Wintrobe, Ronald.

JL65.C66 1991   342.71'03   C91-093861-X

James Lorimer & Company, Publishers
Egerton Ryerson Memorial Building
35 Britain Street
Toronto, Ont M5A 1R7

Printed and bound in Canada

6 5 4 3 2 1 90 91 92 93 94 95

CONTENTS

PREFACE

Ronald Wintrobe
Robert Young

This book contains papers presented at a symposium on
Canada's constitutional future which took place at the
University of Western Ontario on November 9, 1990. It
was organized by the Political Economy Research
Group, of which we are the co-directors. A symposium
is an extended discussion of some subject, where various
speakers address aspects of the topic and where there is
time for opinions to be freely expressed, exchanged, and
developed. The session lasted all afternoon, from 1:30
until 5:30. All six contributors were in attendance
throughout (with the partial exception of Édouard
Cloutier, who arrived a little later than expected). Also,
as the reader will see, there was ample time for participation in the dialogue by the many students and faculty
who attended on that Friday afternoon. This was one of
our major objectives.

The central purpose of the symposium was to provide
an analysis of the present constitutional crisis. It was to
inform Canadians, particularly English-speaking
Canadians, about the current state of constitutional play,
and to point out implications for the future. We felt this
required tackling three aspects of the constitutional
problem: (1) the underlying structure of public opinion
about the Canadian community and constitutional

issues, (2) the economic parameters which could constrain constitutional choices, and (3) the political processes and institutions which already are engaged in shaping our constitutional future. Since the drive for change is issuing mainly from Quebec, we also felt that each aspect of the issue should be addressed by two speakers, one of whom would be especially knowledgeable about that province.

We thought long and hard about whom to invite. Generally, we needed people close to the issue because it is evolving quickly. On the other hand, politicians and public servants did not seem suitable because their positions and personal agendas put limits on how frank they can be. As well, we wanted the analytical depth and historical perspective which academics can provide. So all the people invited were scholars, and of the best sort. Each is engaged enough in the issue to provide good information, yet is detached enough to produce trustworthy commentary. All are constitutional players, but they have been drawn into this matter precisely because they can provide innovative and reliable analysis. (For information on their qualifications, see the Notes on Contributors at the back of the book.) Here, a less formal introduction might be appropriate.

One could call Édouard Cloutier the engaging face of a determined Quebec. He is a big man, with presence and humour. No detached academic, he likes to float among the people, as indeed he must in order to interpret public opinion as sensitively and deftly as he does. Working with the Centre de Recherches sur l'Opinion Publique (CROP), and as an advisor to the government of René Lévesque, Édouard Cloutier was responsible for the polling which underlay the PQ government's referendum strategy in 1980. He was trained at a high-tech American school, the University of Rochester, and is one of the few political scientists who conducts formal experiments: he studies opinion movements. As is apparent from his contribution, Édouard Cloutier is also a strong democrat, with great faith in the people he studies.

Roger Gibbins, of the University of Calgary, knows the West, and is a highly respected student of regionalism, in both Canada and the United States. He has worked for the Canada West Foundation, and currently teaches a seminar with Peter Lougheed, the former premier of Alberta. Despite his work on regional and sometimes radical movements, Roger Gibbins exudes calm and rationality. Precisely because of his measured views, concern for fairness, and good judgement, he now serves as co-editor of the *Canadian Journal of Political Science*. His conclusions at the symposium may seem pessimistic, but they must be taken very seriously.

Pierre Fortin is an excellent economist with an international reputation. But he has also applied his expertise to the most important and difficult questions in political economy — national and constitutional issues — and has been actively engaged in debate, notably as head of an association of economists in favour of a 'yes' vote in the 1980 referendum. He has also worked on social policy reform. Pierre Fortin is a precise, ascetic scholar, in an old Quebec tradition. His rare sense of public service, fine analytic abilities, and prodigious capacity for work have inspired great respect among economists. One of his recent honours is being chosen to deliver the Innis Lecture at the 1991 meetings of the Canadian Economics Association.

Of all the contributors, Grant Reuber has had the most varied career. He is currently Chancellor of the University of Western Ontario, where he served as Chair of Economics, Dean of Social Science, and Provost, establishing a reputation as a talented and uncompromising administrator. He then moved into business, as Senior Economist at the Bank of Montreal, and also served as Deputy Minister of Finance under the Clark government. He returned to the Bank and became President. We were pleased that Grant Reuber agreed to participate in the symposium, not only because of his long involvement with University of Western Ontario, but also because his economic expertise is tempered with the pragmatism of a senior businessman. As he makes clear, Canadians will ignore, at their peril, the reactions of business to the process of constitutional change.

André Blais is hard to introduce. In French he is *un numéro unique*. One of the most original of the new generation of Quebec political scientists, he seeks not to be distracted by received wisdom and superficialities, but to grasp the essential logic of political processes and patterns. André Blais has a deep grounding in Quebec politics, as *'un gars de Drummondville'* and as a student of economic policy and public opinion. He has also ventured far beyond these frontiers into voting studies, electoral systems, bureaucracy and political discourse. He accepted our invitation to discuss the constitutional process in Quebec, then really thought hard about its logic, producing a clear and daring analysis which much impressed those who heard it.

We sought out Peter Russell, not only because he is one of Canada's leading constitutional and legal scholars, but also because he personifies a Canadian tradition of commitment, sophistication, and optimism. He advised the federal government during the Meech Lake process, and his disappointment over the Accord's failure is obvious. Yet just as he always brings enthusiasm, tolerance and insight to academic debates on almost any topic, he is now deploying these qualities to search once more for solutions to the constitutional dilemma. That Peter Russell came to the symposium despite a punishing schedule and heavy responsibilities elsewhere testifies to his commitment to Canada: his contribution shows this passion clearly, along with his rare ability to be constructive and creative in the constitutional minefield.

These six people were brought together by the Political Economy Research Group (PERG), which was established in the Faculty of Social Science in 1988. This group is a loose network of scholars with overlapping academic interests in the application of economic methods to political phenomena, in the influence of economic factors on political processes, and in the political, social and economic effects of public policy. The group is multidisciplinary, and although many of its activities are specialized, PERG also has a mandate to educate students, the public, and the broader scholarly community about important issues. In the summer of 1990, the constitutional crisis was obviously such an issue. The symposium was organized in the belief that informed analysis would help continue a dialogue within and between the Canadian communities, a dialogue essential to resolving the crisis in a rational manner.

The symposium on Canada's constitutional future did do that, in a modest way. The interchanges were lively, the audience was active, there was much good humour, and everyone learned a lot. For its success, we are most indebted to the speakers for participating, and for their quick work in overseeing minor revisions to their texts. We also acknowledge with thanks the consistent support for PERG by the University of Western Ontario through its Academic Development Fund. This symposium could not have taken place without special funding from the Dean of Social Science, Emöke Szathmary, and it gained much from the help of Peter Neary, Bill McClelland, and Joanne

Harbluk. The proceedings were transcribed by Lynda Sollazzo and integrated by Jayne Dewar, both of whom did fine work under severe time pressure. Finally, we wish to thank Jim Lorimer, who saw fit to broaden the symposium's dialogue by making the proceedings available to a wider audience.

INTRODUCTION

Robert Young

When the Meech Lake Accord was rejected, Canada was left in a state of constitutional uncertainty. Although there have been no explosive events since the summer of 1990 and there is as yet no obvious and widespread tension in the country, a crisis clearly looms. The papers gathered here reflect sharply differing viewpoints about the current situation, the options open, and the ways that change will proceed in Quebec and Canada as a whole. But all these papers do make it clear that fundamental constitutional revision is being contemplated in many quarters, especially in Quebec, and that the stakes in this issue are high for all Canadians. They also make it evident that events may move quite quickly.

The papers that follow were delivered in November 1990. They will not soon be dated. Although the participants in the symposium were to focus on the future rather than the past, history sets limits on the pace and direction of change. Some of those limits are analyzed here, as in Pierre Fortin's dissection of the old economic arguments against Quebec independence, and the strong contention of Édouard Cloutier, Roger Gibbins and Peter Russell that extensive public consultation must accompany future constitutional negotiations if their result is to be accepted as legitimate. Moreover, the basic forces driving change will not soon alter, and these are portrayed by some contributors with clarity and great frankness. Roger Gibbins, for instance, shows how the Charter of Rights has allowed latent anti-Quebec sentiment back into the mainstream of political debate, and Grant Reuber is quite blunt in arguing that while business can function profitably under any constitutional arrangement, short-term instability and adjustment costs pose major threats to firms. Finally, several of the contributors make predictions and offer prescriptions. Peter Russell lays out a possible process through which negotiations could take place between Quebec, the other provinces, and Ottawa, in a constituent assembly. André Blais predicts what Quebec's Bélanger-Campeau Commission is likely to recommend and how the Bourassa government will respond. Even if these prognostications turn out to be wrong, it will be useful in the future to ask where and why the supporting analyses went astray.

It seems very likely, though, that these presentations will not turn out to be misguided; instead, taken as a package, the papers give a complete and compelling account of Canada's constitutional dilemma.

Édouard Cloutier begins by depicting the resurgence of support for sovereignty in Quebec in the post-Meech period. There is still the old vagueness about what "sovereignty-association" really means, but more Quebeckers than ever before now support the notion. Moreover, he argues very strongly that a shift has occurred — one formalized in government pronouncements and in the establishment of the Bélanger-Campeau Commission — such that the people of Quebec will decide their future, almost certainly through a referendum. So already, he argues, sovereignty has come to reside in the directly expressed will of the people. He shows that this is also occurring in the rest of Canada, where political elites were unable to push Meech through against popular resistance.

If formal independence has traditionally been supported in Quebec as a means of ensuring the survival and development of a distinctive people united by a shared language and culture, the major arguments against it have been economic. Pierre Fortin shows how these arguments may no longer hold. Quebeckers are now in a position to make political decisions which "come from the heart and not from the pocket book." In fact, a more confident Quebec business class running a modernized economy believes that it is dependent on global, not Canadian, markets, and that federalism now operates as a drag on growth. For Fortin, the new economic argument for sovereignty essentially is that a small, adaptable, consensual society with a loyal business class, and with public policies tailor-made for it, is more capable of success than is the same society when inserted within a larger unit where adjustment is slow, government is inefficient, and policies — because they must reflect an inter-regional compromise — are not quite suited to its requirements.

But what of the rest of Canada? Obviously, the opinions and interests of non-Quebeckers will bear heavily on constitutional change. If Quebec emerges from the process of formulating its position with a shopping list of demands for new powers, perhaps backed up with a supportive referendum result, then there must be negotiations. The outcome of any negotiations, and hence the desirability of various options from Quebec's point of view, will depend on the reaction of the rest of Canada. What is it likely to be?

Here, Roger Gibbins provides some sobering observations. Generally, Canadians outside of Quebec are dissatisfied and sour about the direction of the country.

They have little confidence in the government of Brian Mulroney or in other governments. They have very little interest in renewed constitutional negotiations, and, especially in the West, there is an irritation with Quebec which makes people willing to play "chicken" with that province, that is, willing to call the bluff of assertive Quebeckers. These attitudes are important because, after Meech, it is impossible for leaders alone to design constitutional change. The people must be involved. Yet Gibbins argues that if they are involved, the process will break down in an overload of issues and a welter of conflicting demands. In the past, Canadians have been flexible and accommodating, and non-constitutional innovations have handled many of the stresses in the system. But in the future, if Quebec presents a host of new demands, the mood of the rest of Canada means that the only choice may be between the constitutional status quo and outright independence.

But even if Quebeckers opt for formal independence or for sovereignty-association, there would still have to be negotiations. In the last part of his presentation, Peter Russell offers a sobering list of what would be on the table in the event of a unilateral declaration of independence by Quebec: aboriginal rights, the status of the anglophones in Quebec, the ownership of the northern part of the province, and the national debt. To these difficult matters can be added trade relations, control of a common currency, provisions for the mobility of people, the fisheries, immigration, and many other issues. In short, regardless of what Quebeckers choose there will have to be negotiations about the division of powers between governments and about policy co-ordination.

In this context, Grant Reuber delivers a sweeping review of problems with the current constitutional allocation of powers. The federal system, he contends, has become less effective and efficient over the years. His general prediction is that the country is heading for a substantial decentralization, in order to reflect the differing preferences among communities in Canada, "while maintaining at the centre only those powers and responsibilities in which there truly exist some external economies in providing public goods and services." The bulk of Reuber's paper is a survey of areas of jurisdiction, with analysis of how they might be optimally divided between levels of government so that duplication would be reduced and diseconomies avoided. This is essentially the sort of exercise that would be involved in a rational re-drafting of the whole Canadian Constitution. But whether this will be necessary depends on the position taken by the Quebec government; whether it will be possible depends on the process through which the rest of Canada frames its response. These crucial matters are addressed by André Blais and Peter Russell.

The first response of the Bourassa government to the failure of the Meech Lake Accord was to set up a special Commission on the Political and Constitutional Future of Quebec. It is headed by Michel Bélanger of the National Bank and Jean Campeau, formerly of the Caisse de Dépôt et Placement, the giant public-pension investment fund. André Blais, in a careful analysis, shows why this commission and its co-chairmen are the critical actors in formulating Quebec's position. Rather than concentrating on the great institutional choices of sovereignty or federalism, Blais believes, the commission will tend to focus more precisely on the division of powers. This will allow Quebeckers to unite in favour of the transfer from Ottawa to Quebec of substantial powers, in both the cultural and economic realms. Indeed, the constitutional game in Quebec might culminate rather quickly in a referendum supporting the demand for these powers. Then, of course, a new game would start, one involving Ottawa and the other provinces as well as Quebec.

At this point, Peter Russell makes his contribution. He divides the future process of constitutional politics into three stages. In the post-Meech atmosphere, broad public consultation is absolutely essential, and Russell shows how this is proceeding. The crucial stage, though, is that of concrete negotiating, which cannot be done by consultative bodies. Nor, he argues strongly, can it be done bilaterally between Ottawa and Quebec. The other provinces must be involved. This leads to his proposal for a constituent assembly made up of delegations from the provincial legislatures and the national Parliament. In such an assembly, over a period of several months, a new division of powers could be hammered out. Were strong, representative provincial and federal delegations able to reach agreement on amendments, then the third-stage — ratification — should follow quickly. Peter Russell admits that this process may look bizarre in light of our historical experience, but in the current context it may be the only way to achieve broadly acceptable constitutional renewal. Without some such procedure to manage change calmly, there is a risk of great tension, substantial disruption, and severe conflict. A new and stable order would be reached only after all Canadians had borne very large transition costs.

It will be evident to the reader by now that the Canadian confederation is indeed in crisis. Our collective future is radically uncertain, and probably troubled, to say the least. The presentations which follow depict the several dimensions of the current crisis. Now it is up to each of us — and all of us — to see our way through.

I

The Citizens and the Constitution

1
WE THE PEOPLE: PUBLIC OPINION, SOVEREIGNTY AND THE CONSTITUTION

Édouard Cloutier

This presentation makes three main points. The first one deals with how Meech as a constitutional transformation process has introduced "the people" as a constitutional actor. It surreptitiously but very factually did so. The second point concerns what is going on in Quebec right now with regard to the populace, and the third point concerns what can be expected from the Quebec and Canadian points of view in the longer term, that is, a couple of years from now.

Meech

Basically, Meech has been transforming the constitutional situation in Canada without anybody really saying so. The formal institutions say that we are living under a monarchy, which has been run pretty much by elites ever since Confederation. In the constitutional process related to Meech, however, there is a very clear indication of changes brought about in constitutional practices.

Mainly, we can say that Meech was an arrangement among elites which failed largely, according to most people, because of a unanimity rule. But in my view, it failed mainly because of a very widespread and strong opposition from the people in English Canada. And it also had relatively weak support from the people in French Canada, primarily in Quebec. If popular support had been strong in any way whatsoever in English Canada, Meech would probably have gone through, because elites in Manitoba especially, and even in Newfoundland, would not have blocked the proposal that was on the table if they had known that the people were very much in favour of it. But it was not that way at all. Everybody knew, since all measures of public opinion except one indicated this very clearly, that the people were against the Meech agreement. This is the main reason why leaders opposed to Meech could, without fear of backlash, resort to shenanigans of all kinds, using procedural technicalities for example; they knew that the people were silently cheering their actions.

Not only did the polls indicate that the people were against Meech, but the events in Manitoba and Newfoundland implied "the people" in the most formal sense. The mechanism through which Meech had to go in Manitoba was officially set up so that the voice of the people could be heard before the Meech proposal could be either accepted or rejected. So the name of the people was invoked in the most formal fashion in Manitoba, and the name of the people was invoked equally formally in Newfoundland. Premier Wells said very clearly on the night of the June agreement in Ottawa that he would have to go back to his own people, and maybe hold some sort of referendum, before either agreeing to or rejecting this whole deal. So, the people got into this process in an informal way, informal in the sense that everybody knew from the polls that English-Canadian people were overwhelmingly and steadily against this agreement. Then they got formally into the process in the sense that at least two governments invoked the will of their own people to manage to bring the whole approval machine to a stop. This led finally to the death of the agreement.

Another matter which brought the people forward, and about which not very much thinking has been done, but which is very important, is that in October of 1989 Albertans elected Stan Waters to the Senate of Canada. This followed the spirit of the Meech Lake Accord which said that the federal government would henceforth not name senators without consulting the government of the province from which they came. The Alberta government gave a sovereigntist interpretation of this agreement when it said: "We will go to the people, have them vote and give you the results so that you implement them." This form of applied sovereignty is closely related to Meech since it was during the June agreement in Ottawa that the federal government announced, alongside the formal agreement, that it had agreed to name Mr. Waters as a Senator from Alberta. One cannot but think that this had something to do with dealing underneath the table with regard to the Meech agreement. The result of such a deal is a *de facto* constitutional amendment since it will henceforth be absolutely impossible for any federal government to resist the clearly expressed will of the people with regard to senatorial nominations.

Whichever provincial government uses this formula — that is, having the people vote upon a senatorial candidate in order to come up with a list of nominees — will force Ottawa to designate as senator the person who will have received the most votes. So, very formally, it is a constitutional precedent that the people of a province have in fact elected a senator to the Canadian Senate. Further proof of this comes from the fact that Mr. Waters was somebody who was not liked at all by the federal government at the time, and is no more liked now, indicating that some arm somewhere was twisted politically. On this matter, the federal Conservatives were going against the grain of their own ideology, to say the least. The people of Alberta, encouraged by their provincial leaders, scored heavily against the system by forcing federal elites in Ottawa to accept their own choice.

Generally speaking then, the people actually got their foot into the door of the constitution process even though their name is absent from all formal constitutional documents. The Canadian Constitution will henceforth have to deal with the people, not from Canada as a whole but from specific provinces, for it is they, after all, who have altered the course of the Meech negotiations.

The People in Quebec

Now what about the people in Quebec? Almost all measures of public opinion — twenty-four of them taken since January of this year dealing with "sovereignty," "sovereignty-association," "separation" or "independence" — have come up with record results, regardless of which pollster took the measure or which measure was used. The numbers on independence, separation, sovereignty, and sovereignty-association are the highest on record since measurements started in 1962. With regard to sovereignty and with regard to sovereignty-association, these measures have now topped the 60 percent level. The most recent one indicates a 66 percent approval for sovereignty-association. And there is now very little difference in these scores between sovereignty and sovereignty-association. As far as "independence" and "separation" are concerned, their scores are lower than for "sovereignty" or "sovereignty-association," but they are still at record highs, topping the 40 percent level for separation and the 50 percent level for "independence." These numbers include the English-speaking people who are not too keen on scoring high on these measures, as you know. So even considering English-speaking people, support for sovereignty reached the 60 percent mark sometime in May 1990. We have no measures taken over the summer, but all measures taken since the beginning of autumn are also in the same range.

It is also important to consider how the people in Quebec want to participate in the constitutional process. In the few polls taken in the last years, where the question was asked "Would you like to vote on this?" or "Would you like to have referendum on the constitutional question?" it always produced a very overwhelming "yes." I have seen no score underneath 60 percent on such a question. And even when the question is made more difficult to answer positively, the response is still above 60 percent. For example, it is easy to say "yes" when you are asked "Do you want to vote in a referendum?" But if you ask, as I did back in 1984, "Who should decide on the constitutional powers of the government of Quebec, the Supreme Court of Canada or the people of Quebec in a referendum?" the result still holds. On this question, 66 percent said the "people of Quebec in a referendum" and only 25 percent said "the Supreme Court of Canada." The choice was pretty stiff there, and you had to go against the grain to say a thing like that. And, even though the majority was not always 60 percent, there was a clear majority among all sub-samples — whether isolated by mother tongue, place of birth, age, or education — who thought that the Quebec people taken as a whole were an authority which was superior to the Supreme Court of Canada as far as constitutional affairs were concerned.

Another point about the people of Quebec today concerns the Bélanger-Campeau Commission. Everybody has been very speculative about this commission, its composition and its possible outcomes. Very few people, however, took the trouble simply to read carefully the law which constituted this commission. This legal text is important because it was written jointly by the two main parties in Quebec, which gives great meaning to its wording.

In that text one finds a series of "whereas" which define the parameters to interpret why the commission is constituted to study and report on Quebec's political and constitutional future. The third "whereas" refers to the *necessity* to get a new constitutional status for Quebec. This is the only introductory clause that is a call for action. It asks the commission to come up with a new political and constitutional status for Quebec.

Directly relevant to our topic are the first and the second "whereas." The first, enunciated at the very beginning of the Act, which places it above all other considerations and provisions, says "whereas the Québécoises and Québécois have the right to determine their own future, economically, socially, and politically…." This first clause bears directly on our topic: the right of the people to self-determination. This clause represents a very clear message that the two main political parties in Quebec have given a mandate to a commission to act upon the future of Quebec, considering firstly that the people of Quebec have the right to determine their own future.

The second clause goes further in that it states that there is a "demonstrated will of the people of Quebec to have a direct voice in the constitutional future of Quebec." It commands some form of referendum. There is no other way whereby the people can have a direct say in things if they don't get to the booths and vote on the matter about which they are supposed to have a direct say. So the Bélanger-Campeau Commission has very much to do with the people, at least with the people of Quebec. It is formally ordered to produce a design for Quebec's future, taking into consideration first, the right of self-determination of the people, and second, the fact that these people want to pronounce themselves directly on this at some point in time.

Another point along these lines has to do with how the current Minister of Intergovernmental Affairs in Quebec, Gil Remillard, conceptualizes the constitutional future. In his book called *Le Fédéralisme Canadien: le repatriement de la constitution*, published in 1985, he criticized what had happened in 1981-82 in the following manner.

> The people of Quebec, holders of sovereignty, have not been consulted with regard to this re-patriation, nor has anyone else in Canada. It is difficult to understand how a democractic country like Canada has been able to amend substantially its constitution without any kind of formal consult-ation with its people.

That is what he said before becoming Minister of Inter-governmental Affairs in 1985. Since then, as Minister, he has been instrumental in the Meech Lake deal. (We note in passing that the Meech deal contained no provi-sion regarding the people of Quebec or of Canada, so it seems that Mr. Remillard was not too keen on applying his own principle.) Last summer, however, he gave an interview to *Le Devoir* in which he said, "The last word about the future of Quebec will have to come from the people of Quebec. We must have the political strength to get what we want to get, and this political strength rests entirely on one will, the clearly expressed will of the people of Quebec." It is the basis of legitimacy, he says.

> My only reference, my basic reference, is the people of Quebec. The contract which we will propose to Ottawa, the people of Quebec will have decided. We are not at the mercy of the rest of Canada. We are here as a nation, as a society capable of taking our own responsibility and affirming what we are.

So the actual minister, a specialist in constitutional affairs, and the main individual decision-maker about the constitutional process, has clearly indicated that the people will speak about their future.

The Future

The third point follows from this. We are headed towards a referendum on some form of sovereignty in Quebec. If both major parties can agree on this, the people will respond in an overwhelming, massive fashion to this referendum. What form will it take? I do not think sovereignty will mean outright independence or separation. As a social scientist, I shouldn't make too many predictions. But it seems that, in the most formal sense, a new constitutional actor will be introduced in the whole Canadian constitutional debate. That actor will be the people of Quebec considered as an entity, one speaking directly on these matters. This should not be seen as a new thing in light of the fact that the people of Alberta have already voted to elect their own senator, and that it was in the name of the people of Manitoba that so many procedural matters were set up in the legislature, in the meanders of which Meech slowly sank never to re-appear. So a sort of precedent has been created here, one which is going to be brought to some kind of a crest. Of course, there is nothing wrong with that. As a Quebecker and a democrat, it seems to me that this is a perfectly sane thing to do: since the French and the American revolutions, democratic constitutions say very clearly that sovereignty belongs to the people.

The introduction of the people as a constitutional actor will bring about a saner way of looking at everything, at least in Quebec. Up until now, we have only been talking about the sovereignty of the government of Quebec, as though a government was sovereign in itself. But a government doesn't produce its own power, constitutionally or legally speaking. The power must stem from somewhere else, which is God, or the Queen, or, since the French and American revolutions, the people.

It seems to me that the sovereign, if anything should be sovereign, should be the people and not the government. So the sovereign can decide, and once this is understood, then it is evident that the sovereign — the people — can decide to have its own affairs run by two different governments. If an individual can have two different companies to run its affairs — or three or four for that matter with regard to your car and your house and so on — the sovereign people could have its own affairs run by two, even three, or four levels of government, if it sees fit. The difference would be that if there is ever any quarrel between all these governments who are running the people's affairs, there will always be one way to settle the quarrel: put the question to the sovereign. The sovereign will say "That is enough: this government does this and that government does that, and I don't want to hear about it for the next 50 years or so." There will be a boss somewhere who will finally say the definitive word at some point in time.

Clearly, we are entering into a period where the voice of the people will be heard more and more, and not just in Quebec, but also in Canada. In the process, the People will inscribe themselves formally as a constitutional actor in Quebec and in the rest of Canada.

2
CONSTITUTIONAL POLITICS IN THE WEST AND THE REST

Roger Gibbins

In this short contribution I present a simple, perhaps even simplistic, argument. I try to show that the nature of public opinion outside Quebec acts as a constraint on constitutional politics in Canada. Indeed, I argue that the nature of public opinion and the demand for public participation in the constitutional process will pose such a constraint that they will lead to the collapse of the constitutional process. That is the bad news. The good news is that a collapse of the constitutional process may not be such a bad thing, and, indeed, may well be one of the best options we have in Canada.

Let me begin by sketching in the nature of post-Meech public opinion in Canada outside Quebec. It should be noted, incidentally, that public opinion polling outside Quebec on constitutional issues is different from public opinion polling inside Quebec, because inside Quebec every poll is seen as part of a run-up to what may eventually be a referendum on the future of Quebec. Therefore, the bottom line becomes very important in Quebec public opinion polling; it predicts the political future in a very specific, focused way. Outside Quebec, pollsters are interested more in questions of mood, of the general drift of the country, because fortunately there is no referendum in sight.

What, then, is the character of that mood? Well, let me give you a few snapshots first, then offer some more general commentary, and then discuss why the mood is important for understanding constitutional politics. The snapshots come from a public opinion poll released by the CBC and the *Globe and Mail* in the autumn of 1990. It was based on a large sample, with almost 2300 Canadians sampled from coast to coast.

One question asked, "Should the federal government and the provinces start new negotiations to try and find a constitutional compromise acceptable to all the provinces or should the federal government and the provinces put constitutional matters aside and get on with other matters?" We find that across the country 39 percent say start again, while 56 percent say put it off and let's get on to other things. There is very little regional variation here, except that as you go further west in the country, the hostility to new constitutional negotiations increases. And, if you look at Reform Party supporters in western Canada you find that 70 percent of them are saying "Let's get on with other things, let's shut the constitutional process down." I would argue here that as the recession sets in, and if the recession is as bad and as long as we think it is going to be, then the level of interest in constitutional politics will sink even further.

A second question asked, "How satisfied are you with the direction the country is heading?" Not surprisingly, almost 80 percent of Canadians are dissatisfied, and most of them are very dissatisfied. The interesting thing, however, is that *satisfaction* is greater in Quebec than it is elsewhere in the country. In this and in a number of other questions, Quebec emerges almost as an island of contentment in a sea of dissatisfaction with political institutions in Canada. Of course, when I mention to my friends in western Canada that Quebec is relatively satisfied, their response is "Well, so they should be, it's their government." Although these questions are not on the specific constitutional character of Canada, it is important to recognize that the political unrest or discontent that they tap is very pervasive in the country as a whole.

The third question produced no surprise. "What do you think of the job Brian Mulroney is doing as Prime Minister of Canada?" The response "very good" or "good" was given by 22 percent; "poor" or "very poor" was the response given by 75 percent. In Quebec, the Prime Minister, naturally, is doing quite well. Only 50 percent of the people there disapprove of Mr. Mulroney. Outside Quebec the numbers are staggering: 85 percent in Ontario, 83 percent in British Columbia, and 87 percent on the Prairies feel the Prime Minister is doing a poor or very poor job. In fact, on the Prairies more than 50 percent say Mr. Mulroney is doing a *very* poor job. This finding is important for the constitutional debate because it indicates the absence of effective national leadership in the run-up to a new round of constitutional negotiations. In addition, it is worth noting that, at least in western Canada, the premiers themselves have also been damaged by the Meech Lake process, and are now reeling from a very unsympathetic and hostile public environment. A recent poll in Saskatchewan, for example, showed that Grant Devine was even more unpopular than Brian Mulroney. A staggering result!

There is one more snapshot worth mentioning before moving into the more general constitutional picture. People were asked, "How confident are you that the present federal and provincial leaders can resolve the present constitutional difficulties in Canada?" The answers were "very confident," with less than 1 percent of the respondents so replying; "confident," with 20 percent; "not too confident," with 51 percent; and "not at all confident," with 26 percent. The greatest level of confidence was in Quebec, and the lowest level of confidence was in western Canada.

How, then, do we characterize the general public mood on the eve of new constitutional negotiations? What is Keith Spicer going to encounter when he goes out to see what Canadians really think? First of all, there is a general sourness, or nastiness, to the public mood. There is no faith in politicians or in existing political institutions. There is no sense of confidence in the ability of governments and leaders to handle the situation that we are in. Secondly, there is resistance to renewed constitutional negotiations, and that resistance will grow as the recession deepens, and, perhaps, as we face war in the Middle East. The third point is that there is little sense of a constitutional crisis. There is such a sense among political scientists, but when you dig very deeply into the public opinion data, it is not clear that the public believes that there is a crisis. Or, if they are aware there is a crisis, they are largely indifferent to the outcome. In the CBC/*Globe and Mail* poll people were asked what they thought the likelihood would be of Quebec eventually separating from Canada. Outside Quebec, only about 10 percent think that is an ultimate possibility; 6 percent on the Prairies; 10 percent in British Columbia; and 10 percent in Ontario. I would not say that this reflects a realistic assessment of the chances of Quebec leaving — not at all — but it is an important finding because it contributes to a willingness on the part of the Canadian public to play "chicken" with the nationalist movement in Quebec, a willingness, perhaps, to call the bluff of the nationalist movement in Quebec. This is a dangerous willingness, I suspect, but it exists nonetheless, and it is particularly evident in the public opinion data from supporters of the Reform Party in western Canada. They are the people who think Quebec is not going to go, and they are the people who are digging in their heels the hardest.

Perhaps the best way to characterize public opinion is to say there is a sense of fatalism about the country. There is a sense that the constitutional process will play itself out in Quebec, that we outside will see eventually what happens, and that we will take it as it comes.

Here it is important to consider the impact of the Charter of Rights on the constitutional discourse in English Canada. The Charter has had two very negative effects on constitutional rhetoric in English Canada. First of all, and this is particularly evident in the West, the Charter has legitimized a subterranean anti-Quebec, anti-French settlement that was always part of regional politics. Prior to the Charter, people who were opposed to Quebec, or who were opposed to bilingualism, French, metrification, or whatever, were more or less pushed off the public stage because their opposition was delegitimized by political elites within the country. What the Charter has done, however, is to endorse that discontent and to bring it back into mainstream political discourse. People who in the past simply disliked Quebec can now wrap themselves in the flag of the Charter and come charging forward in the defence of universal human rights. People who prior to 1982 were merely bigots are now defenders of universal human rights, and they have altered the nature of constitutional discourse; the Charter has given them a very powerful platform from which to oppose the constitutional aspirations of Quebec. The Charter has also affected the constitutional debate by injecting the language of rights into constitutional politics. Rather than elaborate on this point, I will simply mention that rights are very difficult to deal with because they tend to be non-negotiable. Thus, when a constitutional debate is framed in terms of non-negotiable rights, the process can break down very easily.

What is the significance of all this? So what if the public is in a foul mood? Does it matter? I think it does because of the fallout from the Meech Lake Accord. Two very important lessons were learned from the Meech Lake Accord. The first is that the public must be involved in the constitutional process. Even the first ministers, as they appeared for press conferences during the final week of negotiations on Meech Lake, were quick to point out that in the future we must never handle constitutional reform this way again. So the public must be involved.

The second lesson is that if the public is involved, they will so overload the constitutional agenda that the whole process will break down. Public involvement makes sequential constitutional reform impossible. There cannot be, for example, another "Quebec round" in the constitutional process. The public's involvement in the constitutional process makes that all but impossible because people are unwilling to put off, and thus subordinate, their demands to an uncertain future. Aboriginals will not wait until "next time," nor will Senate reformers in the West. But if there can't be a "Quebec round," can there be an "everything round"? It is doubtful. Anyone who imagines that Quebec, Senate reform, aboriginal rights, and the federal deficit can be rolled into one tidy constitutional package should wake up and smell the coffee. But so too should someone who believes that we can tackle these things sequentially. We can't. So we have, then, a somewhat difficult choice. We can fall back on an illegitimate, non-public process, which would probably not be acceptable to Canadians, or we can adopt a public process that won't work. This leads to the rather bleak conclusion that we have a situation of constitutional gridlock or meltdown in Canada.

There is, perhaps, a bright side to this. It is at least arguable that the collapse of the constitutional process may not be a bad thing in the long run, although it is extraordinarily risky. It may be time to give up on this uniquely Canadian belief that there is a constitutional fix, if not necessarily a quick fix, to political problems. Maybe we should abandon that hope, and maybe we would be better off on a non-constitutional playing field. Looking, for example, at the relationship between Quebec and the broader Canadian federal state over the last thirty years, roughly from 1960 to 1990, it is clear that very little constitutional headway was made in altering the relationship between Quebec and the rest of the Canadian federal state. In fact, many Quebeckers would argue that we have made even negative constitutional progress over those thirty years. However, during that same period we have made a great deal of informal progress or non-constitutional progess. The federal system has turned out to be very flexible. Once we get away from the Constitution itself, we become quite creative, quite imaginative.

It may be the case, then, that the lesson to be learned from this history is that constitutional progress is very difficult; indeed, in the post-Meech environment, it is going to be even more difficult to achieve than it might have been in the past. So it might be advisable to abandon the hope of finding a constitutional response to Quebec. The Constitution and federalism are not infinitely flexible. There are theoretical and practical limits to the extent to which we can alter the nature of the Canadian federal state. It has turned out that the constitution is not flexible enough to accommodate the Meech Lake Accord, and therefore there is little reason to suspect that it will be sufficiently flexible to accommodate the new conditions or demands that are coming out of Quebec. Nor is it likely to be flexible enough to accommodate the huge menu of constitutional reforms that the public hearings will pull on to the Constitutional agenda.

There is, incidentally, a parallel here between Quebec and the West that is worth noting. In western Canada the recent holy grail of constitutional reform has been Senate reform. Western Canadians are insistent about talking about Senate reform. And the reaction, naturally, of people outside the West, is to say "Look, come to your senses, a triple-E Senate is not in the cards. Why do you keep talking about it? Why do you keep banging your head on the wall? The Constitution is not going to change to accommodate the triple-E Senate."

Non-westerners are right, and western Canadians should abandon the idea of a triple-E Senate. But the broader lesson is that the Constitution may not be adaptable to the demands of Quebec either. This leaves us, then, in a very risky and somewhat scary situation. Quebec may well decide, for all sorts of legitimate and appropriate reasons, to go. It seems, however, that this is a risk we may have to take because a constitutional solution is going to be so difficult to get to. It is going to be difficult primarily because the process is now public, the constitutional agenda has been greatly expanded, and we are in a situation of constitutional overload. It may be time, then, that we return the politics of national integration to the back rooms where they belong, and take them off the constitutional agenda. Ultimately, Quebec must decide what its own future will be. But the realistic choice may be between the constitutional status quo and independence. To repeat the point, the only realistic option may be to muddle through with the Constitution that is now in place, or to admit that the Canadian experiment has failed. The middle ground of constitutional amendment has disappeared into the bog of Meech Lake.

INTERCHANGE

Question to Roger Gibbons:

Western Canada is hypocritical. People there take a
strong stand against the federal government but they
rejected the Meech Lake Accord, which gave them more
power. Can you explain this hypocrisy?

Roger Gibbons:

It would take a long time to explain the hypocrisy of
western Canadians. Let me try to do so by linking it back
to the presentation of Édouard Cloutier. There is no
doubt in my mind that the Meech Lake Accord found a
great deal of support among provincial governments in
the West. In fact, it could have been written as easily in
Edmonton as in Quebec City, or perhaps even Ottawa.
However, it is also clear that the western Canadian
public sees the country somewhat differently than the
provincial governments do. If western Canadians had
the chance to act publicly in the constitutional arena,
they would not want to do so within the confines of
provincial communities. To most western Canadians, the
dominant political community is the national political
community, and the reason the Accord ran into trouble
was because it was seen, accurately or not, as threatening
that national community. So I would argue that provincial governments in western Canada were badly out of
step with public opinion within the provinces. That
showed up within Alberta, for example, where the provincial government supported the Accord from day one
to the end, right down the line, and public opinion polls
within Alberta showed the Accord with as little as 8 or
9 percent support, and close to 90 percent opposition. So
there was a clear discontinuity between provincial

governments and the population. Whether that is hypocrisy or not, I'm not sure, but it is a clear political tension in the West.

Question to Roger Gibbins:

What is the difference between those in the West who don't think Quebec will separate — that is to say those who are playing "chicken" — and those who have become so indifferent to the process that they say, "If Quebec wants to go, let them go." What is the significance of this distinction with regard to the place of Quebec in constitutional negotiations in the future?

Roger Gibbins:

Again, I'm not sure there is a very clear answer. I would try to segment public opinion into three categories, and I can do this only in a qualitative way. I think there are people who are prepared to play "chicken" with the nationalist movement in Quebec, in the sense that they are prepared to *confront* the constitutional demands coming out of Quebec. They are still a relatively small minority in the West, although they have found a very articulate voice within the Reform Party. Secondly, the dominant mood is one of indifference or resignation, a belief that the dynamics of Quebec's future will be played out within Quebec. That is really the community that will make the decision, and the rest of the country will simply pick up the pieces as it sees fit after that time. Thirdly, there is the dwindling minority of people who sense that there is a real problem with Quebec, and who will push for some kind of positive accommodation that will bridge the constitutional aspirations of Quebec and the existing federal state. That seems to be the group that is shrinking.

Question to Édouard Cloutier:

Some of us who have been sympathetic to Quebec nationalism are a little suspicious of the Quebec corporate interest in the Meech Lake Accord and in free trade with the United States. Certainly in Quebec, among the francophone population, there has been dissent, I think, by groups like Solidarité populaire about how Quebec corporate interests seem to be stepping into the breach left by English-Canadian corporate interests. To what extent is Quebec popular opinion in favour of some sovereigntist option also in alignment with the social agenda of the PQ of René Lévesque? Or is there a negative correlation between concern for a progressive or a socially informed Quebec future and sovereigntism?

Édouard Cloutier:

I think that the movement has been as follows with regard to the last part of your question. In the 1970s, it was very clear that there was a close association between sovereignty and left-of-centre politics in general. That changed somewhere around 1984-86: some of the sovereigntists have been moving to the centre, and then maybe a bit to the right of centre; and some of the people who were not sovereigntist, but who were already on the right of centre, have become sovereigntists. We are now in a situation where, for all sovereigntists taken as a whole, it's not clear whether you would find a majority right or left of centre. It would probably split in two. I don't know where the majority would be. In fact, the whole society has been moving more to the right in Quebec, and I suspect that Ontario has now moved to the left more than Quebec, in the last few months at least. So you must not look towards Quebec for new thinking for the left; Ontario is the place for this right now.

The thinking in Quebec with regard to sovereignty now is that, for any forward move to be made, there has to be some sort of a national front. There has to be the acceptance that if there exists something that is Québécois, it must be shared by everybody, no matter what his or her origin. There is also the acceptance by a great number of people that it is better to do your sovereignty if you have the bourgeoisie behind you than if you don't have the bourgeoisie behind you. It is the only way to do it for some of the people who would otherwise worry, saying, "My God, we just can't be born without a bourgeoisie — that's like being born without a backbone or a heart or something."

Now they are reassured on this. We have a bourgeoisie, we have built it up and it looks pretty healthy, and it seems to be going towards sovereignty. The Bélanger-Campeau Commission seems to be ready to move that way. But one never knows what happens with these things.

Going back to what I said before, the bourgeoisie may not really have a choice, because if they don't put their stamp on it, they are going to be overwhelmed by the people, who score very high on support for sovereignty. A poll in the newspaper yesterday was 66 percent in favour, including English-speaking people whose score is about 12 percent. So it means on the French side, it is something like 70 percent. I don't know if you saw the flags in the streets on June 24th last, but there were lots of them, and if the system doesn't...*accouche*, as we say in French, it means give birth...if the system doesn't give birth to something, the people in the streets will give birth to something which will not be much to the liking of the elite which runs the system right now. So I don't think the commission has the choice. I think they will have to *accouche*.

Pierre Fortin:

I would like to ask Édouard about his experience with the impact of the economic situation, meaning a recession? This is something everyone except Michael Wilson sees. What impact is this going to have on the willingness of this popular opinion movement in Quebec to go as far as if there were no recession? In other words, recession is a time when you don't like change of any sort. Am I right, or can you say something else to which you would attach some probability of being true?

Édouard Cloutier:

Generally speaking, with regard to Quebec nationalism, I think that what you were saying is right. The nationalist feeling got its boost when the times were good economically, and when the times were more difficult, as in 1981-82, support for independence declined somewhat. So there can be a peaking off of nationalism. But if you look at what happens in other countries, it seems that there is a point at which, when things become too bad, then it has the contrary effect. Nationalism could become, if things were really very bad, a rallying point for some sort of very popular movement with revolutionary outlines. Now, I don't see this coming about. The only point I want to make is that when things go bad economically, generally speaking, it dampens this kind of movement; but if they do go really bad, then they can trigger something else at some point in time. But I don't see it coming about now.

II

The Economy and the Constitution

3
HOW ECONOMICS IS SHAPING THE CONSTITUTIONAL DEBATE IN QUEBEC

Pierre Fortin

Introduction

The current search for a new constitutional order by Quebec is a political reaction to a political event, the rejection of the Meech Lake Accord. However, economic considerations are already playing a crucial role in the political debate, and are likely to exert a major influence on the context of the new constitution. As editorialist Alain Dubuc has recently observed, Quebec has clearly entered the post-romantic era where it is getting down to the practical business of defining exactly what sort of new constitution it wants.

The core of this paper aims at explaining why and how economic events and ideas are in fact shaping the constitutional debate in Quebec. To begin with, in previous rounds of constitutional debate in Quebec, the drive for a greater measure of sovereignty was constantly restrained by the general apprehension that any such occurrence would reduce the province's average standard of living. The main arguments were, first, that Quebec's economy was internally weak and highly dependent on external ownership, finance, manpower, and technology; second, that any unilateral move by the province to appropriate greater constitutional powers would meet with swift trade retaliation from outside; and third, that Quebec drew substantial net economic benefits from its participation in the federation.

Today, all three arguments stand on their heads. First, the perception is spreading that Quebec is not so dependent on the rest of the Canadian economy, and that its dynamic business class and highly-educated manpower have allowed it to bridge its traditional productivity gap with Ontario. Second, after the Free Trade Agreement with the U.S. and the many rounds of GATT negotiations, the point is well understood that trade retaliation against Quebec is no longer a serious possibility under any constitutional option, and that the economic fortunes of countries have become less and less dependent on political size and status. And third, the widespread view now is that Canadian federalism is such an economic failure that it threatens to "Argentinize" Canada in general, and Quebec in particular. I shall examine the three arguments one by one.

Quebec's Economic Self-Reliance

The first reason why no measure of economic threat is now likely to dissuade Quebec from following the political course it sees best fit to meet its political objectives is that the province now understands it has all the human, technological, and financial bases it needs to generate its own economic development as a mature member of Canada and the world community.

TIME SavingsVoucher

Almost 55% OFF the Cover Price.

Name _____ Apt. No. _____

Address _____

City _____ Province _____ Postal Code _____

Mail this Savings Voucher today and you're entitled to get TIME at only $1.33 an issue—a savings of almost 55% off the $2.95 cover price. Just tell us how many months of TIME you want.

☐ 2 years
(104 issues)

☐ 1 year
(52 issues)

☐ 6 months
(26 issues)

☐ Payment enclosed.

☐ Bill me later.

(Example: 6 months at $1.33 an issue is $34.58 — GST not included.) The cover price is $2.95. Rates good in Canada only.

© 1988 Time Inc.

TIME MAY 13, 1991

1CAH524

≡

TIME
THE WEEKLY NEWSMAGAZINE
P.O. BOX 1776
ADELAIDE STATION
TORONTO, ONTARIO
M5C 2P6

Canada Post Corporation • Société canadienne des postes
44418

Thirty years ago, francophones in Quebec were poor and illiterate. According to the census of 1961, their relative status in their home province was exactly the same as that of black Americans in the United States. Both earned 64 percent of the national average income. Over half of francophones aged 20 and over had not reached grade 8 in school, and only 2 percent of young people went through university education. In spite of being 80 percent of the Quebec population, francophones owned only 20 percent of Quebec manufacturing and 47 percent of the total commercial sector. Quebec's productivity lagged 15 percent behind Ontario's.

Since then, two-thirds of the productivity gap with Ontario has been closed. Almost all teenagers go through grade 8, and over 20 percent make it to university education. About 40 percent of Quebec university students are in business schools, and they constitute 45 percent of all business students in Canada. The income gap between francophones and others is currently no more than 10 percent. An enterprising, outward-oriented, and pro-free-trade business class has blossomed. They now own 40 percent of manufacturing and 62 percent of the total commercial sector. They run 27 of the 50 fastest growing companies in Canada, they spend more on research and development than anywhere else in the country, and they have been in the avant-garde of financial innovation in Canada throughout the 1980s. This progress has also been encouraged by strong social cohesion, close cooperation between the provincial government and the private sector, improved business-labour relations, and a more competitive tax system. The provincial government has focused on supportive economic policies, and is helping to make Quebec opinion and institutions self-reliant, market-oriented, and competitive as well as cooperative.

Economic and Political Boundaries

The second reason for the greater economic self-confidence in Quebec under any constitutional scenario is the contemporaneous trend toward bilateral and multilateral free trade in goods and capital. Forty years ago, with tariff walls around countries higher than 40 or 50 percent and widespread capital and exchange controls, political and economic boundaries tended to coincide. Nowadays, with world financial deregulation almost complete, and after several rounds of multilateral and bilateral tariff reductions such as GATT and the Canadian-U.S. Free Trade Agreement, capital is almost perfectly mobile across countries, the remaining tariff barriers are few, and non-tariff barriers are coming under attack.

There are two major implications. First, economic space is no longer limited by political boundaries, and standards of living are basically independent of population size. For example, in 1985 the correlation coefficient between income per capita and size among OECD countries was -0.10 and statistically insignificant. The size of the Quebec economy is actually equal to or greater than that of Austria, Belgium, Denmark, Finland, Norway, New Zealand, and Switzerland, and not much smaller than that of Sweden. The second implication is that even under the most pessimistic scenario, trade retaliation by Canada against a hypothetically independent Quebec is unlikely and would at any rate not be very effective.

Economic Failure of Federalism

The third reason why more sovereignty is no longer seen as a threat to standards of living is the widespread conviction that federalism is an economic failure. There are three supporting reasons: (1) the federal debt is out of control; (2) monetary instability is destructive of jobs and competitiveness; and (3) federal development policies have failed. The general presumption is that the situation reflects not merely bad policies, but also a bad system, one which is incapable of correcting its wrong course. Hence the need for constitutional reform.

(1) The Federal Debt is Out of Control

The federal debt has increased from 15 percent of national income in 1981 to 40 percent today. The debt is now $200 billion higher than if this explosion had not occurred. The problem originated from loss of control over program expenditures at the end of the Trudeau era, and it has been inflated further by the record high interest rates of the last few years. In the past decade, we have experienced faster debt accumulation than every other large industrial country except Italy. Applying a hypothetical return of 10 percent per year to these $200 billion of excess debt translates into an annual income shortfall of about $20 billion for Canada, or $2000 per family. The debt makes us all poorer. Furthermore, interest payments on the debt now crowd out federal spending or crowd in federal taxes at the annual rate of over $10 billion just to prevent the problem from getting worse.

The contrast between the failure of the federal government to control its deficit and the success of Quebec government in achieving budget balance is striking. This clearly adds to the relative discredit in which the central government is held in the province.

(2) Monetary Instability Destroys Jobs and Competitiveness

In Quebec and in other parts of the country, public opinion is also outraged by the high interest rates and exchange rates that are imposed by persistent monetary restriction. In the last year, real interest rates have exceeded 9 percent, and they have been 5 percent higher than in the U.S. These high interest rates have been a major factor behind the 25 percent appreciation of the Canadian dollar against the U.S. dollar since 1986. As a result, Canadian manufacturing firms have never been so uncompetitive in North American markets since data on competitiveness began to be collected forty years ago. Monetary policy in this way is delaying and even destroying a substantial proportion of the benefits anticipated from the Free Trade Agreement.

Also hard to take is the fact that in spite of rising unemployment and bankruptcies, inflation is not yet clearly under control. The GST is coming, and another oil crisis looms. Perhaps the monetary authorities will raise the national unemployment rate to 14 or 15 percent, if necessary, to reduce the inflation rate from 4 to 0 percent.

It is hard to convince the average businessman that this makes sense. The frustration is not only with the policy itself, but with the seeming inability of the government to realize that the game plan does not work, and that something else should be tried which could keep inflation effectively under control and avoid the astronomical costs of recessions, bankruptcies, and unemployment. The recent Annual Review of the Economic Council of Canada has attempted to face the problem constructively by suggesting that consensus-based inflation control might help solve the quandary. The council's suggestion is probably being laughed out of court as naïve and irrelevant, in disregard of the fact that social cohesion may be one of the major systematic elements associated with good economic performance in modern industrial countries.

(3) Federal Development Policies Have Failed

The final source of frustration with economic federalism is the perceived failure of development policies, mainly in the areas of manpower, research and development, and financial market regulation. All three are absolutely crucial under the current pressure for global competitiveness, and yet among industrial countries Canada ranks among the worst performers at least in the first two instances.

One of the reasons may be that under the present constitution the federal government is permitted to spend in almost every area it wants. The constitution allows it to spend in its own areas of exclusive jurisdiction, in areas of shared responsibilities, in all areas not explicitly defined by the BNA Act, and also in areas of exclusive provincial jurisdiction. The result is a monstrous system of competitive government, replete with duplication, contradiction, and waste. Twelve years ago, Senator Arthur Tremblay and two colleagues at ENAP produced evidence showing that out of a total of 465 federal and provincial spending programs in Quebec, 277 (or 60 percent) were directly or indirectly overlapping.

Manpower, research and development, and financial market regulation are just three examples of this absurd administrative mess, which are mentioned here only for their key importance to economic growth. The Quebec business and labour community has long found that in these three areas the provincial government has generally adopted policies which they view as more sensible and better-adapted to the specific Quebec environment than federal policies. Hence the flood of current proposals for constitutional amendments which would give Quebec full control.

These considerations underline the more general principle that the new Canadian constitution should make a major attempt at minimizing the overlaps between jurisdictions. The duplication and waste generated by the current constitution is clearly substantial, and it has certainly contributed to the current financial distress of the federal government to the extent of several billion dollars.

Conclusion

The economic failure of federalism on the fiscal, monetary, and economic development fronts is the subject of wide consensus in Quebec. One major implication for the constitutional debate is that the traditional defence line of federalism, based on the "obvious" economic benefits of the present system, is in very serious trouble. It is not credible any more. The fear now stems from the fact that the federal government currently operates as a major drag on the economies of Quebec and of the entire country. Hence the reference to Argentina. The Prime Minister is right to state, as he did recently in Mont-Saint-Anne, that "the economic foundations must be completely solid." But this is precisely the point: many in Quebec are so clearly convinced of this truth that they want to change or opt out of the present failing system before it is too late.

Actually, business opinion is even more radical. Earlier this year, a SOM-Les Affaires survey of 200 business leaders from the province's 500 largest industrial firms found that those who believed political independence would have a positive impact on the long-term economic development of Quebec outnumbered those who thought the impact would be negative by a 4-to-1 margin. This suggests that no degree of political independence for Quebec is believed economically more dangerous for the province than the way the federal state is now run in Canada.

To summarize, the most important difference between the current constitutional debate and that of 10 years ago is that Quebec sovereignty is now more clearly perceived as an economically credible and viable option. Average business opinion goes as far as believing it would enhance the long-term economic prospects of the province. This is reinforced by the view that, even under the worst political scenario, it is unlikely that the Canadian common market will be dismantled. Quebec will obviously want to remain part of the Canadian dollar zone, but it could have its own credible and viable currency if forced out.

The broad political outcome is still uncertain, but the foregoing analysis indicates that the province will want to put an end to the era of competitive government. It will push for a sharp clarification, with minimum overlap, of the legislative and spending responsibilities of the two levels of government, and for wide control over key instruments of economic development such as manpower, immigration, research and development, communications, trade and financial regulation, transportation, regional development, and income security. It will also seek greater control over the Bank of Canada by the regions, and greater exchange rate stability. It may even go as far as asking that constitutional restrictions be imposed on the power of governments to borrow.

Whether this will take place in a much more decentralized federation, in a community of quasi-sovereign regions with delegation of powers to the central government, or in a sovereign Quebec state will depend on interests, but also on emotions, on goodwill, on capacity to communicate, on strategy, and also, obviously, on chance. Needless to say, everything would have been much simpler if Meech had made it through.

4
FEDERALISM AND NEGATIVE-SUM GAMES

Grant L. Reuber

In the heart of every Canadian lurks both a separatist and a centralist. The separatist favours local autonomy in order to have maximum freedom to take advantage of local opportunities and to cater to particular preferences unencumbered by collective constraints. The centralist favours a collective approach in many areas as a means of dealing with issues more effectively, efficiently and equitably, and also as a means of building a nation of international significance. Because of our history, wide regional diversity, heterogeneous population mix, vast distances and the relative isolation of many communities, this separatist/centralist tension has been greater in Canada than in most countries. And over time, depending upon circumstances, the balance has shifted.

Centrifugal Forces

In recent decades, centrifugal forces in the country have grown relative to centralizing forces. One factor has been growing affluence. An increasingly rich society has been able to afford the cost of indulging its regional preferences and idiosyncrasies.

Another factor has been the evolution of "big govern-ment." Questions of who pays and who gains, public choice and decision-making have become much more important, as have the constraints enforced by the centre on the regions. These issues have been difficult to re-solve effectively through a political process that today remains much the same as when government was much smaller and simpler.

A third major centrifugal force has been the much closer integration of Canada with the world economy and particularly with the North American economy. Because of this, the central government's powers have become more limited, restricting what can be accom-plished through central government action.

A fourth factor, which has become important during the past decade, has been the huge and persistently rising public debt of Canada. Servicing this debt today absorbs about 35 percent of all federal government revenue and this ratio shows every sign of rising further in future. As a consequence, the financial capacity of the federal government to support its existing activities, to say nothing of new initiatives, has been seriously impaired and may get worse before it gets better. Moreover, the heavy return flow of debt service payments from the federal government has substantially altered the picture of the flow of funds between the federal government and the regions.

An underlying notion of federalism is that there are external economies in providing certain public goods and services through a central government, e.g., national defence, foreign policy, a common currency, economic stabilization policy, and controls on environmental spill-overs. The federal government's comparative advantage lies in areas where there are such external economies. Provincial and local governments can deal equally well or better with other responsibilities. In a rational world, the aim would be to allocate functions to those levels best suited to discharge the responsibility, and to have close collaboration at the edges where responsibilities meet. In a political world motivated by power, influence, and money, this is wildly unrealistic.

What we have instead is widespread government duplication of activities by at least two, and more commonly three or four, levels. All vie with each other for popular support at the taxpayers' expense, frequently with little or no apparent benefit accruing to the citizen. Add into this mix a set of highly organized vested interest groups and one has all the ingredients for a never-ending series of negative-sum games, i.e. diseconomies. The resulting cost reflects not just the expense of running this complicated process but, more important, the cost entailed by semi-paralysis, poor decisions, and public frustration. Minority interests, as often as not, overrule the priorities of the majority. Public reaction, not surprisingly, is disenchantment and a sense in some quarters that the external diseconomies of federal government activities now frequently outweigh the external economies.

Business Implications of Constitutional Changes

One of the difficulties in considering the business and economic implications of different constitutional options is that there are innumerable options and all are ill-defined at this stage. I will start, then, with business interests, narrowly defined.

The essential feature of business activities is that they are voluntary activities motivated by the prospect of profit. As such, they are highly adaptable to whatever circumstances present themselves. In the end, the test of whether business activities occur is not whether the activity is generally beneficial but whether it yields a return to the owners of the factors of production comparable to what can be earned in some other activity or in some other place. Thus if the economy is organized in a highly inefficient way, for example because of tariffs, regulations and other market impediments, business can and will still function profitably. The cost of the inefficiency is essentially borne by the public. The owners of the factors of production, at least those that are mobile (e.g., labour and human and physical capital), will require a competitive rate of return, or they will simply go elsewhere or do something else.

If business is relatively immune in the long run to whatever constitutional changes are made, the same cannot be said of the short run. Instability and uncertainty greatly bother business and generate negative economic consequences, irrespective of the arrangements eventually agreed upon. Because of instability and uncertainty, business decisions will require a higher risk premium, will tend to have a short time horizon, and will be far more cautious than if such decisions are made within a reasonably stable constitutional framework.

In addition to the added cost of instability, if constitutional arrangements are substantially altered, there is the further cost of readjustment to the new arrangements. For example, new arrangements may require separate corporate entities in various jurisdictions, or the establishment of separate production or marketing facilities, or meeting different regulatory requirements, and so on. All this entails costs.

While business can pretty well pass on any long-term costs of constitutional arrangements, it is more difficult to assess and pass on the costs of instability (because of their inherent uncertainty) and the costs of adjustment (because in the short run many costs are fixed).

Economic Implications of Constitutional Changes

Most businessmen, as responsible citizens, are, of course, concerned with much more than simply the narrow impact of constitutional changes on their business. Various attempts have been made in the past to estimate the economic costs and benefits of Confederation as it stands in comparison with separate self-governing regions. For a variety of reasons, all have had only very limited success.

What would be the likely economic consequences for the regions if Canada broke up? The evidence suggests the following broad conclusions:

1. There probably would be a significant cost for most parts of the country, but separation would not spell economic disaster.

2. The heaviest burden would fall on the poorest regions of the country. Whether there would be an economic cost to central Canada is less clear.

3. The economic cost would be highest for all parts of the country in the short and medium term, especially if the break-up was abrupt, acrimonious and disorderly.

4. The longer-term costs would be greater to the extent that separation gave rise to merchantilistic nation-building policies within the regions, so impeding their economic integration into the rest of North America and the world economy.

A major uncertainty arises in connection with federal government assets and liabilities. How these were divided would not only be highly controversial but also would have a significant impact on the outcome.

Decentralization

While it is doubtful that the country will break up, all signs point to substantial decentralization of power from Ottawa to the provinces. Had it been accepted, Meech Lake would not have ended the process. Rather, it would have brought Quebec fully into the process which then could have more effectively handled the continuing evolution of decentralization. Without Meech, the process is stalled, which presumably is what the opponents of Meech intended.

When the process is reactivated, the decentralization of responsibility for economic policy and control over the instruments of policy will be a central issue. What is sought seems to be as much decentralization as possible to reflect differences in circumstances and preferences among communities, while maintaining at the centre only those powers and responsibilities in which there truly exist some external economies in providing public goods and services. Associated with this is the desire to establish greater fiscal responsibility by re-emphasizing that each government has the responsibility itself to raise the money it spends. What does this mean in terms of specific policy areas?

Traditional Areas

(1) Money and Currency

Money and currency at present are unequivocally within federal jurisdiction. Over the years the federal government has allowed the provinces to infringe seriously upon these powers by permitting provincially-chartered institutions into the payments system, the deposit insurance system and so forth. Financial market regulation is further complicated by provincial jurisdiction over stock exchanges. If the proposed federal legislation for financial institutions is adopted, it is doubtful that there will be much pressure for further decentralization of financial regulation. We will effectively have a dual system with collaborative arrangements between the two parts, rather than an integrated federal-provincial system or a federal system.

As for monetary policy, appeals for regional policy and participation by provincial authorities in executing monetary policy are not new, but they continue to lack credibility. This is mainly because of the high mobility of capital, nationally and internationally. Strong central control and management is needed if the country as a whole is to have any policy independence at all.

The references sometimes made to the regional character of the Federal Reserve System in the U.S. ignore the fact that the regional banks have little or no influence on national policies and are mainly concerned with local economic developments. One may also question how much regional governments would welcome the participation of a federally-based central bank in matters dealing with regional policies.

(2) Internal Free Trade and Factor Movements
Substantial internal barriers remain to the free movement of goods, services, capital and people within Canada. Removing and reducing these barriers is essentially a collaborative exercise in which the federal government has and could continue to have an important leadership role. In a more decentralized country with weakened federal powers and influence, the ability of

the federal government to promote the elimination of these barriers would be reduced. Conceivably, however, the provinces could collaborate to do this without a federal government. For example, recently the Maritime Provinces have begun talks amongst themselves about establishing a common market.

(3) Foreign Trade, Investment, Immigration, Transportation and Communication

What about the traditional areas of "National Policy" — foreign trade and investment, immigration and transportation and communication? Since first devised in 1870, these areas have changed considerably, and conflicts with the provinces have become more common. Although provincial governments today play a much more important role in these areas, the federal role remains dominant. Moreover, because of the interdependence among the provinces and the interface with other countries, these are areas where the federal government would appear to have a continuing comparative advantage in making and executing policy.

New Policy Areas

Issues become much more complex and uncertain when we leave these traditional policy areas and look at the newer areas that have emerged since 1945. For convenience these may be grouped into five categories:

(1) Resource policy

The central questions here are, first, who should control the environmental and other regulations governing resource development; second, how should the rents from resources be shared among shareholders, miners, processors, the province and the people of Canada generally; and third, what if any role should federal subsidies have in financing regional resource projects? While provincial policies dominate in this area, deeply divisive conflicts continue to arise.

Bargaining power rather than logic is the main factor determining the sharing of rents and subsidies. The danger is that a tug-of-war between the contending parties will result in less or more than the optimum level of investment — a negative-sum game. Perhaps the answer lies in some formula, agreed upon in advance, for sharing resource rents and for subsidizing large resource projects.

The environment also may be considered common property in which all Canadians, present and future, have a stake. Leaving environmental decisions entirely in local hands might result in a systematic bias, via the competitive process, towards less satisfactory standards than would result from an unbiased system. At the same time, national standards are likely to deny local citizens the right to choose their own environmental trade-offs. In this situation, special-interest pressure abounds, and the end result can easily be worse than if either local or central priorities prevailed. The recent fracas over dams in the West and the impending row over phase two of James Bay illustrate how divisive this issue has become.

(2) Regulatory activities

The same is true of the web of provincial and federal government regulations found in virtually every sector of the economy. Sorting out regulatory conflicts could take a variety of forms, depending upon particular circumstances. These might include, for example, deregulation by either level of government, or adoption of the same or similar regulations by both, or explicit compensation to a province for economic damage attributable to federal regulations; and so forth. All of these could reduce duplication and possible external diseconomies.

(3) Stabilization policy

Fiscal, monetary and debt management policies remain the principal means available for stabilization purposes. In the best of circumstances these policies have only limited effectiveness; and to be effective at all they have to be run by the central government. Apart from consultation and advice, the provinces have little to contribute to improving either the execution or effectiveness of stabilization policy. More often than not in the past provinces have, in fact, run pro-cyclical rather than anti-cyclical policies. Macro-economic policy intrinsically is less vulnerable to vested interests than micro-economic policy, and therefore is less vulnerable to negative-sum games.

(4) Income support and redistribution policies

Exactly the opposite is true of income support and redistribution policies. These are among the most complicated and controversial policies that governments confront. They entail transfer payments from the federal government to provincial governments as well as transfers made directly to individuals. Among the many difficult issues posed are the following:

to what extent should central priorities dominate provincial priorities and preferences?

to what extent have these programs made some provinces excessively dependent upon the federal government?

to what extent have such programs contributed to regional disparities?

At bottom, the question is whether the federal government should largely vacate this area, providing money and tax capacity to the provinces to take up the slack, perhaps on a per capita basis, and letting the provinces largely run these programs as they see fit. Greater local autonomy would cater more effectively to local needs but would give rise to greater unevenness in such programs among the provinces.

The scope for vested interests to turn the federal-provincial process dealing with these issues into negative-sum games is enormous. For example, the present combination of federal and provincial income-support measures results in absurd penalties on the working poor. Moreover, producer subsidies such as agricultural price supports, which are really only income support measures, bear unusually heavily upon the poor and substantially offset other forms of income support.

(5) Producer subsidies and regional development subsidies

Few areas have aroused more controversy than the large federal subsidies provided to support various enterprises, projects and activities across the country. Most of these are uneconomic. Federal subsidies are normally supported on such grounds as regional development, environmental control, supporting small business, promoting research and development, and so on. But interest groups dominate the play.

As one writer has said, "As the state takes over the market, so interest groups take over the state and mandarins are left with little room to manoeuvre. With the market depressed and the elite overwhelmed, no effective check resists the clamoring interests." And, one might add, in a federal state this gloomy picture is even darker.

Conclusion

The first conclusion to be drawn from all this is the possibility of a more centralist approach can be dismissed without much discussion as being unworkable and unacceptable. The options then seem to be:

(i) the status quo with an attempt to reduce duplication, ambiguity and the scope for negative-sum games; that is, a more effective and efficient federal system; or

(ii) a confederation of much more autonomous regions and a central government whose responsibilities are limited to well-defined areas and subject to regional checks and balances, something comparable in many ways to the EEC.

The trouble with the first option is that over the years, instead of becoming more effective and efficient, the federal system has become less so. And so far no one has come up with a satisfactory way of fixing its deficiencies. The second option, on the other hand, while removing or reducing some of the problems of a federal approach, essentially changes the entire face of Canada, and undermines its status and potential as a nation.

INTERCHANGE

Question to Pierre Fortin:

Mr. Fortin, your view is largely the view of the Quebec business community, and that was the thrust of your presentation. Is there in fact a consensus around this agenda that you have set out? Do Quebec workers agree with your diagnosis?

Pierre Fortin:

Some of it is clearly business only. The labour movement is obviously less ready to argue that big deficits in government are a very important problem. But there is consensus on the fact that world free trade helps Quebec in making its political decisions on political foundations only, and makes the economic consideration much less important than otherwise. This is a widespread perception and conviction. Then, there is also a very large consensus, and outside the business community too, about the new business class and the highly educated manpower being able to run the Quebec economy. Although here, it is quite important to observe that the employment performance of Quebec is still wanting, compared to the productivity performance. But it is quite natural to expect that, because any region or country that is trying to catch up with the frontier of productivity in the world, like, for example, New England twenty years ago, or now East Germany, first of all starts by having faster productivity growth and, at the same time, lags in terms of employment. When it reaches the frontier then employment starts to follow. This is a standard pattern. But there certainly are diverging views here on whether the Quebec economy is doing fine overall or if there are some very weak spots. Employment is a weak spot, and will be for perhaps a number of years to come. So, on the debt, labour groups and business groups may disagree, but they do agree that monetary instability is bad, and they do agree that federal development policies have failed.

Question to Pierre Fortin:

You mentioned that recently federalism has been a problem for completing the development of Quebec — it has impeded the region. But is it possible that there is not a structural problem with federalism but rather a management problem at the federal level?

Pierre Fortin:

There are certainly many reasons, other than federal development policies, why Canada lags other industrial countries on the level of research and development performance, on the level of manpower planning, development, and upgrading. Obviously. But what is seen is that those factors pile up on perhaps other structural factors to make things worse. Essentially that is what is happening.

Question to Pierre Fortin:

When you speak of political sovereignty for Quebec are you talking about complete political independence or of maintaining some kind of political ties with the rest of Canada?

Pierre Fortin:

I keep my own opinion for the voting booth. My father told me that you shouldn't speak about politics or religion. That is the best way to make enemies. But what I am saying is that the economic factor in the constitutional decision-making process now is becoming less and less important, although it is clearly being given prominence in the debate. For example, Mr. Bourassa has constantly emphasized that first of all, it is of the utmost importance to have economic stability, and he constantly emphasizes the need to protect that and to enhance that. The opposition leader in Quebec is a first-class professional economist. The two co-presidents of the Constitutional Commission are top Canadian financiers. And the commission itself is heavily loaded and tilted toward the business community. So it is quite clearly a basic message that the central pre-occupation of the debate will be with economics.

There are many reasons now pushing people to be much bolder toward sovereignty than before, because those factors I mentioned which worked very strongly to inhibit seeking this objective are much less operative than in 1980. Actually I wrote a book in 1980 saying that sovereignty-association was entirely viable for Quebec and, of course, nobody believed me at the time, and they all voted no. Although, my own point was meant to be essentially non-committal. At this time I have not changed my mind. I think that political decisions on the future of a country should come from the heart and not from the pocket book. And I have maintained this opinion. But although I am maintaining the same position as in 1980, there are a lot of people who are going much farther than I am ready to go now; in other words, I was in front of people in 1980, but now I am in back of many others who are ready to be more radical than I can be. This increases the likelihood, the political likelihood, of a much more decentralized federation, or of a community-like confederation, or of a sovereign Quebec. I don't know what the outcome will be, but certainly the trend of my argument is precisely that.

Grant Reuber:

I just wanted to add that the achievements of Quebec in catching up are important. It's also conceivable, of course, that with a sorting-out of functions and a better functioning system, the rest of the country would be better off as well. So the incentives, such as they are — and I don't think they're critical to this whole question — are such that if functions were sorted out, and you had better federal government in a broad sense, the rest of the country would also blossom under that arrangement. So it isn't just Quebec that stands to gain from that possibility. Of course this depends on the rest of the provinces picking up and doing the right things. It's not obvious that it would work that way, but it could work that way.

Pierre Fortin:

The difference in Quebec is that this feeling has a very strong psychological impact on the debate, and that is my point. But you are obviously right.

Question to Pierre Fortin:

Are we looking, in your opinion, at an alternative to transfer payments for have-not provinces? Is the solution in your opinion a total deregulation of the situation which is supposed to entice foreign capital and other capital to come in? Is that what you are saying would be a more viable solution than transfer payments or what would you say?

Pierre Fortin:

I think you have put your finger, on what, to me, is the most important problem. The closest to my own feeling about Canada is that federalism is sharing, and the Quebec debate takes place entirely outside these considerations. The reasons for this are very egotistical, in a sense: it is simply that Quebec is now realizing that its balance of costs and benefits in terms of national accounts are essentially zero with the federal government. So they say, well, we receive a lot of equalization payments but on the other hand Ottawa spends much less in Quebec for other purposes, and therefore our balance is just zero so why not opt out? In other words, this is an additional reason for not being afraid of economic reduction in standards of living, and opting out.

I agree that in any future decentralization of Canada, and in any form that you could imagine that Canada could take, this would be absolutely one of the central questions to discuss. Actually, I worked for a month-and-a-half with the Quebec Chamber of Commerce to help them prepare their brief to the Bélanger-Campeau Commission (trying to restrain them a little bit), and I realized that they were completely — not insensitive, on the contrary — but they really didn't know what to do about these equalization problems and transfer problems. They really have not solved the problem in their minds.

Question to Pierre Fortin:

When we talk about increased decentralization, one of the things that we can say is remotely possible, even though we have had some doubting in the country, is that at least there is some underpinning notion that the provinces that do better can help to put into the pot and give to those who are not doing well. If we see the country beginning to break down into what we could call sovereignty association or more broadly, states that are essentially independent, so that although we share a common currency and we have a common flag, there is really nothing more in common than that between us, then I think something incredibly tragic is happening in terms of the Canadian experiment. If we think that opening the doors and allowing foreign capital to come in, deregulating economies, and allowing people to become pockets of independent sovereign-associated countries is the solution, then I think we have a very serious problem.

Pierre Fortin:

But Grant made a very important point when he talked about this problem in his presentation. He mentioned that the equalization and transfer payment system we have should clearly be questioned in terms of its long-term effects on receiver provinces. I know Atlantic Canada from having gone there and worked there a bit, and through going to conferences on the economies of Atlantic Canada, and what strikes me most in those provinces is the sense of absolute dependence you see there. On the one hand, you would like to help people who have lower incomes and are behind economically, but on the other hand, it is also true that to receive all this manna from heaven induces dependence. In Prince Edward Island and Newfoundland the ratio of the surplus they get from the federal government to their own economy is 30 percent; it is 20 percent in Nova Scotia and New Brunswick, and 10 percent in Saskatchewan and Manitoba. But the problem is worse, as you said, in Newfoundland and areas like this. What are we going to do to try to distinguish between support of people who are in trouble, but at the same time maintain the incentive system for people to get out of this black hole of poverty?

III

Government Strategies and the Constitution

5
THE CONSTITUTIONAL GAME IN QUEBEC: OPTIONS, INTERESTS, STRATEGIES, OUTCOMES

André Blais

What I propose to do in this paper is to look at the process of constitutional reform in Canada as a game. I want to show what the implications of that approach suggest in terms of the likely outcomes of the process. I make some predictions about what various actors are likely to do and also about what all of this will lead us into. More than predicting, however, I am interested in trying to understand several questions. What are the major options in constitutional change? Who are the main actors, the ones who really count in the game, and why? What are their interests, their positions, and what kind of strategies are they likely to adopt in this game?

The Options

So let's start with the options. Spontaneously, Québécois tend to think of there being basically three constitutional options. This is also the way pollsters have defined the issue in recent times. The three options are: (1) federalism,

(2) independence, and (3), in between, sovereignty-association. This is the standard conventional wisdom in Quebec. It is important to understand that this is the way the debate is structured. This affects the whole debate, and it affects the strategies the actors are likely to adopt in the game. One interesting implication of this way of structuring the debate, is that sovereignty-association looks like a very attractive option. It is the middle category. It encapsulates the desire for change — substantial change — and at the same time looks reasonable, and not too radical. It is not as radical as independence. As a consequence, nationalists in Quebec try to preserve that way of defining the debate, and opponents attempt to structure it differently.

It is important to understand what this formulation leaves out of the debate. I would argue that the constitutional debate basically involves two issues. The first is institutional and asks "What are the basic political loyalties of Québécois? What is our identity?" The standard typology (federalism, sovereignty-association, independence) refers to that dimension. Are we basically Québécois? This means that we have to opt either for independence or sovereignty-association, first sovereignty then association. Or are we also Canadian? In this case we opt for federalism, probably reformed to some extent, but federalism nevertheless.

But there is also a second issue that is raised in the constitutional debate, and that is the division of powers. How much power should be left to the government of Quebec? How much power to the rest of Canada, whatever the structure? On this issue we don't have a good way to summarize the options. We know there is a continuum, but we don't know exactly how to define the options, and most importantly, it is not the usual way we define the debate. But I think that we have to take this into consideration when we look at how the various actors define the debate and take their positions. One of the decisions these actors have to make in deciding how to move in the debate is whether to accept the traditional typology or to try to structure the debate differently.

The Actors

The most important actor in the constitutional game, perhaps surprisingly, is a duo — the co-chairpersons of the commission on Quebec's constitutional future, Mr. Bélanger and Mr. Campeau. These two individuals will have a big impact on what is going to develop in Quebec, at least in terms of Quebec's position in the constitutional round.

They have one clear interest — producing a common report that looks serious and credible. They share that interest. It is very clear that if they fail to agree between themselves the commission will be perceived as a big failure and their own reputations will be hurt. My first prediction, then, is that they will indeed produce a common report at least between the two of them. It is very important to understand that it can hardly be different because they obviously lose if they don't agree.

The second observation — and prediction, also — is that these two chairpersons will call the shots. They will decide on the overall thrust of the report. They can afford to do so because they are the two most legitimate members of the commission. If they are seen as having reached a consensus between the two of them, they will more or less force the rest, or a substantial number, of the commissioners to ally with them. Once they have decided where they will move, they will start to make some deals with other commissioners. The important point is that the chairpersons are in a position of strength and should be able to convince a good number of commissioners to ally with them.

My third prediction is that the commission's report is likely to have a great impact on the actual position taken by the Liberal government in Quebec. This prediction is based on two major considerations. First, the public mood. There is in Quebec a great longing, a big search for consensus. At the same time as there is a strong nationalist feeling, there is also a great willingness to make compromises so as to come up with a single position to present to English Canada. There is a desire not to fight old battles again, but to try to come up with the position that will appear in English Canada as *the* dominant position within Quebec.

The other factor that will make the commission's report quite important and influential is the very peculiar position in which Mr. Bourassa finds himself, to which I turn shortly.

Mr Bourassa, the Premier, is the second most important actor. Assuming that he will remain Premier until at least the summer of 1991, here are a few observations. Mr. Bourassa feels most uncomfortable about the Constitution. He would like not to discuss it, he would prefer the issue would go away, to vanish. Mr. Bourassa is also very conservative. And his own preferred choice will be to change the Constitution as little as possible. Finally, Mr. Bourassa is very much attuned to public opinion. He follows polls very closely and is plainly aware of the strong nationalist feelings in Quebec. Consequently, he is deeply torn and ambivalent on the issue. And because he is deeply ambivalent, he is probably very dependent on the commission's report.

The commission is very much his commission. He has been personally involved in the nomination of commissioners. So I think it would be extremely difficult for him to turn down the commission's recommendations. I therefore predict that the Liberal Party will more or less adopt the commission's major recommendations.

The third major actor is the business community. Pierre Fortin has already shown the real importance of the business community in Quebec, and he is quite right, they have a lot of political clout these days and will have a very important role to play in the constitutional process in Quebec. However, despite what seems to be a strong consensus, a sense of self-confidence, and also a great willingness to show itself as being open to all kinds of options, there are substantial divisions within the business community. Small business, as we can see in the brief presented by the Chamber of Commerce, is very strongly nationalist. At the same time, the Conseil du Patronat is very strongly federalist, even more so than it appears. Big business cannot afford to show how strongly federalist it is. Because of the public mood — the necessity of appearing to be open-minded — it has to declare itself open to all kinds of solutions publicly. But privately, big business would very much like to keep things as they are.

An interesting question is why does big business react differently from small business? The first interpretation that comes to mind is simple: big business is more tied to international markets, and so is less likely to be nationalistic. It is more concerned with the world economy, while small business in Quebec is more closely tied to the local economy and so perhaps more nationalistic. However, I don't find this interpretation compelling. It seems there is a consensus within the business community in Quebec for opening the market, for really trying to have an open economy where business can thrive, and there is no difference in the views of small and big business on this count. We have seen the same attitudes in the debate on free trade where there was no major difference between big and small business. So, the major reason for big business being less nationalistic in Quebec these days is that it is tied to a network of associations in Canada. They are more involved in the Canadian community, and they are strongly attached to the Canadian community.

The fourth and last actor is the native people of Quebec, who will play a very important role for two reasons. The first is that they have a legitimate claim to sovereignty. This is exactly the argument that Québécois have been using, that we are a nation, and we can be sovereign if we decide to be. If we have to be consistent, we must acknowledge that the native peoples have the same right. So the fact that native peoples are likely to use that argument makes the whole discussion much more complex.

The second reason, which I think is even more important, is more along the lines of *realpolitik*. The native people form a group that can be easily mobilized, that can resort to all kinds of actions if we don't heed their views, and that can disrupt the whole economy. We know this very well now, since Oka. So we don't have any choice; we've got to listen to their positions. What will be the native people's position in the game? Most of the nationalist Québécois hope that they will be divided, because some nations, the Mohawks in particular, are more integrated into the English-Canadian community, while others are more tightly knit into the Quebec francophone community.

A lot of nationalists hope that these divisions will emerge. However, it is more likely that the native peoples will be able to overcome their divisions and will come up with a strong and united position. They will have a very important message, which will be that any discussion of new constitutional arrangements will have to involve them as a major participant. They will say that if there are to be discussions about new arrangements between Quebec and the rest of Canada, the discussions have to be broadened to encompass the relation between native peoples, Quebec and Canada.

There is a latent message in here as well, which is that any discussion of constitutional reform is going to be extremely difficult, long, tedious, and complex. But the fact that the native peoples are a major actor makes the federalist option more attractive. This is because renewed federalism, contrary to sovereignty-association, does not necessarily entail an overall re-evaluation of the social contract with native peoples.

The Strategies

Now let's come to the most difficult question. What will be the commission's recommendation? In attempting to answer that question we have to try to put ourselves in the perspective of the commissioners. What will they try to achieve? What are the constraints? What kind of game are they playing? The commission chairpersons, in particular, want to produce a report that will be perceived to be well done, serious, and articulate. And I think that the following conditions have to be fulfilled in order for the report to be received in such a fashion. First, the report must show that it is sensitive to public opinion. It must have, therefore, a nationalist overtone, with a demand for greater powers for the Quebec government. Secondly, it has to appear to be to appear non-partisan; that is, not to be linked too closely to either the Liberal Party or the Parti Québécois. And thirdly, it has to provide a rationale for all the positions it is going to take. It has to come up with an underlying philosophy.

Assuming that these are the considerations that the commissioners will have, how are they likely to approach their task? The basic strategy they will adopt is to put the question as much as possible in technical terms. They will try to avoid the partisan, explicitly political, aspects of the question. And the best way to do it is to focus on the second of the two dimensions of the issue referred to earlier — the division of powers. In order to appear non-partisan the objective has to be to avoid framing the issue in terms of the standard classification, of grave institutional options, which is linked in people's mind to the parties. Traditionally, sovereignty-association is associated with the Parti Québécois, and federalism with the Liberal Party. So as much as possible the commission will try to avoid these labels, and the best way to avoid the labels is to move to another dimension, to turn to the division of powers, and to ask the question, "Which powers should be given to the government of Quebec, which powers should be shared with other governments and which powers should be given to other governments altogether?"

Already there are clear indications that this is precisely the route the commission is going to follow. It has approached 100 experts in Quebec and has asked each of them to write a 20-page brief in which they respond to eight questions. I think the way the commission has put the questions is very indicative of the approach they have decided to take. The first question they put to these experts is "What are the main problems in Canada concerning the Constitution?" Then the very next question is a question about the division of powers. "What are the domains in which government of Quebec should have full competence or share competence with other governments?" The next questions concern the impact of having these powers on the maintenance and promotion of Quebec identity, and on economic well-being in Quebec. It is only down the list, in fact, at the penultimate question, when the experts are asked to consider the larger institutional implications of this division of powers.

The commission has decided, very astutely, to first consider the abstract question, the non-partisan, apolitical question of the division of powers, and to consider the issue from scratch. It will try to come up with a rationale to decide on which basis some powers should be given to the government of Quebec and others to other types of government. There are standard tools in the literature for this, especially the tradition in public finance which deals with the optimal division of powers. The commission will probably use that literature in a very special way. It will start with the assumption that whenever in doubt, the decision should be to give power to the government of Quebec. There will have to be strong reasons to shift powers from Quebec to the federal government or to any other kind of government. So the thinking of the commission will be focused first on the division of powers, and it will come up with recommendations for very substantial transfers from the federal government to the provincial government, along the lines that the Quebec Chamber of Commerce has already suggested.

For some time, I expect, the commission will discuss only the division of powers, leaving the question of institutions for the end. It will decide on a substantial transfer of powers to the government of Quebec. It will then face the issue of institutional options. At this point they will reach a deadlock, because there is no conceptual approach that can really help the commission come up with some reasonable technical answer as to what kind of institutional framework Quebec should adopt.

By then the commission won't have much time left. As a consequence, at that stage the strategy will be essentially political. Having pleased the nationalists by recommending a substantial transfer of powers, I expect that the chairpersons will reach out for the federalists and recommend decentralized federalism. That section of the report is likely to be weak and evasive, but it will nevertheless allow the federalists to come on board.

The Liberal government will probably accept the recommendations of the commission, especially as they will be framed in terms of renewed federalism. The nationalists, the Parti Québécois especially, will be in a difficult position, but will probably, in the end, support the recommendations of the Commission having to do with the transfer of powers, while expressing their disagreement about how to get there.

In such a context, the optimal strategy for the government would be to have a referendum in which the question would be put in such a way that it would be supported by an overwhelming majority of Québécois. (We can assume, here, that the government is concerned first and foremost with presenting a unified Quebec position to English Canada.) From that perspective, the ideal question would be one dealing with the transfer of substantial powers to the government of Quebec, while remaining silent about the institutions and the process. After the referendum, a new game would start again, involving not only Quebec but also the federal and provincial governments, as well as native peoples.

6
THE FUTURE PROCESS OF CANADIAN CONSTITUTIONAL POLITICS

Peter Russell

My subject is the future of constitutional politics in the country. I start with the threshold issue of whether we should even go ahead with another round of constitutional politics, given that a majority of Canadians have said they would rather not. Even about fifty percent of Quebeckers have said that and I am part of that majority.

Constitutional politics are extraordinarily dangerous, and they are likely to pull this country apart. They are usually about symbolic things — questions of justice and identity — and we don't have a clear consensus on these matters in this country; on the contrary, we become very divided when we discuss justice. During the Meech Lake process, in debating the Charter of Rights versus the distinct society clause, there was such a polarization for many Quebeckers: they either took our charter or their distinct society. We know that wasn't the real choice, but that is the way these issues get presented and that's why they divide us.

As well, constitutional politics will distract us from very pressing problems in the economy and in the environment which are more gripping in terms of real human need and welfare. Constitutional politics will distract us from those issues, and make our current economic situation somewhat worse. As a tenured professor, and one who is very well paid, I really don't think I can encourage the country to go on and do something that is going to hurt a lot of people who, unlike me, are not tenured, who are not well paid, and who are tremendously vulnerable. Our unemployment rates are climbing, and these people are going to get badly hurt. They are not in this constitutional debate, most of them, and I am sorry that we are not dealing with their immediate problems.

However, there is a momentum, a tide in our affairs, which is running so high that despite all this, we are going to go on and enter into a round of constitutional politics. So, I've decided to be either naïvely positive or, perhaps, positively naïve, and try to figure out how we can handle our constitutional politics better, since we are going to play the game again.

First Nations

Well, something we can do right off the top is to deal with one constitutional issue immediately. We are already dealing with it rather incompetently, and that is the question of aboriginal rights — of the constitutional rights of our aboriginal peoples. We are negotiating with aboriginal peoples right now in various ways across the country, primarily through land claims agreements, but also through some treaty renovation processes in Ontario and in the Maritimes. We can do much better at the land claims process. I was part of a federal task force that examined that process in 1985 and made many recommendations on how to make it work more effectively. These recommendations have been largely ignored by the federal government.

But one thing you should all know about land claims agreements is that in 1983 we made the first change in our constitution since patriation, the only time we have successfully amended our constitution since 1982: the amendment had to do with aboriginal rights. One of the changes made through that amendment was that any rights or agreements put into a land claim settlement become part of the Constitution.

Negotiating land claims is a piecemeal process. But given the very different circumstances that native people are in across Canada, I think that this is the process we should try now. We must try to work it a whole lot better in British Columbia, in the North, in Ontario, in Quebec, and in the Maritimes. There are many unsettled land claims that should be resolved. I'm not saying that the piecemeal land claims process is a surrogate, a substitute for overall redefinition or clarification of aboriginal rights in the Constitution, but we should not hold up progress in dealing with those who were here first, on whom we pushed ourselves and who have never chosen by consent to be part of our body politic, until we have settled all the other constitutional issues facing Canada. We should give priority to aboriginal issues because that is where our greatest constitutional injustice lies, and we should get on as best we can with that right away.

Quebec

What about the great question of Quebec and other constitutional grievances, particularly the western one of being exploited by the power of central Canada? We are at least going to have to deal with the Quebec grievance after Meech. I suggest there are two possible ways of dealing with it. One is to deal with this next round within the existing rules for changing the Constitution — the rules we adopted in 1982 and which maintain legal continuity. The second way is to go outside those rules, to wing it outside the rules of the Constitution.

I will deal here mainly with the first — trying to work within the Constitution Act 1982 — because I am frightened about winging it outside those rules. It is clear that those formal rules are very tough to work with. We learned that at Meech. But we have got to learn how to make them work a little better for us.

There is one point that we all agree upon: all Canadians who are involved in this constitutional discussion, Quebeckers, people outside of Quebec — everyone — all say the constitutional process must be more democratic and open. It can't be a narrow, elitist process. That's motherhood. We are not even debating that one anymore, although it isn't going to be easy to get agreement if we open up the process; it's going to be exceedingly difficult. Now, how do we work the rules of 1982 in a more open way? Well, the way to think about it is in terms of three stages. The first is the period of public consultation and discussion. The second is the negotiation of constitutional proposals, and the third is ratification.

Consultation

Let's start with public consultation, the stage that has actually begun. It has begun in Quebec with the parliamentary commission which André Blais told us a great deal about and also with the Quebec Liberal Party's committee which has been consulting at least the members of that party since April. We also know a process is under way in New Brunswick. We understand Ontario and Alberta are thinking about cranking up some kind of committee or commission to consult the people of those provinces on the constitutional future of Canada. And, of course, most recently, we know that at the national level there is the Spicer Commission, the Citizens' Forum, which was established just last week. There will likely be other consultations set up by other governments, and in addition many privately sponsored meetings on Canada's constitutional future.

Now, the first thing to notice here is that we didn't do this kind of thing before Meech Lake. Even in other rounds of constitutional change, as in 1982, and other changes before that, there was very little of this broad public discussion. The closest analogue you would get to it is the Pépin-Robarts task force in the late 1970s, but it was more like a royal commission: it didn't have nearly the bite that this round of constitutional consultation is going to have, nor the amount of tension and interest it is going to excite. So this is certainly opening up the process.

You are all here today, and, if you are interested in this problem, you're going to be doing a lot more of this in the next eight or nine months. The question is what can be achieved by this type of process, or Mr. Spicer's process, or the process in Quebec? Well, we should be clear about what it won't achieve. It won't draft constitutional proposals. That is not what Spicer's about, and that is not what the Bélanger-Campeau Commission is about.

None of these is set up to draft proposals. They are not negotiating constitutional proposals. We are not at the negotiating stage. So what will they do? They will identify options, objectives, and principles, which come closest to having a consensus support behind them in the particular constituency, or jurisdiction they are working within.

Now, of course, the danger is that if each consultation proceeds within a watertight compartment, so that the New Brunswickers don't have any regard for what is going on in Quebec, Quebeckers don't have any regard for what is going on in Ontario, and Ontarians don't care about what Albertans are talking about, and so on, then this will polarize our situation instead of identifying the grounds for a posible consensus. The biggest onus is clearly on Mr. Spicer, head of the national commission, to try to make sure that all those who are involved in public consultation, including Quebeckers, are at least listening to what others outside of their province, and outside of their region, are dreaming about in terms of constitutional visions. Even though the participants in these discussions are not negotiating (and Quebeckers are particularly adamant about this now), they should be listening to each other — unless, of course, one's constitutional aspiration is the break-up of Canada, in which case all you should be doing is sending intelligent scouts out to figure out what opposition there might be from the federal armed forces and so on, after the independence option is realized.

But Quebeckers who want even sovereignty-association, let alone a more decentralized federation (which seem to be the two key alternatives to outright independence) should be listening to Canadians outside their province, and *vice versa*. Canadians outside Quebec who are interested at least in trying to maintain some semblance of a Canadian union, should listen very, very carefully to what is going on in Quebec. Again, if you have given up, and want Quebec to go, then close your ears now.

Negotiations

Now that is stage one, the stage of consultation with the public. What about stage two? Well, the negotiating stage will begin within a year. The Quebec commission has to report in March and there might well be a referendum some months after that. Spicer doesn't finish up until June, and his commission is crucial in trying to see whether there are grounds for a consensual constitutional agreement between Quebec and the rest of Canada. The public consultation would be over by this spring, next fall at the latest. The question, then, will be what are we going to do in terms of negotiating some constitutional proposals.

Now, we know what not to do. What we used to do is what we are not supposed to do now. What we used to do is to get the first ministers to have a meeting to see if they could work out some proposals. And we know that is out: that can't be done.

Another way of moving ahead into the negotiating stage has been proposed by Mr. Bourassa. It is equally out of the question, and the sooner he learns this the better. His thought is that he will go to Ottawa, having a referendum result which is positive, and he'll negotiate something with whoever is the prime minister next fall.

Now those of us in English Canada, outside of Quebec, can help Quebeckers not dig themselves into thinking there is that kind of process available. No prime minister in Ottawa, Mr. Mulroney or anyone who replaces him, will have either the legal or political authority to cut a deal with the premier of Quebec that will bind the rest of Canada. We in English Canada, as it's called, want to be just as democratic about our constitutional politics as Quebeckers, so there is not going to be a top-down prime ministerial dictate of a deal with Quebec for the rest of Canada. We must get that one off the table quickly, just like the first minister's conference.

What we have to do for the negotiation of proposals is stage a conference of representatives of the constituent legislatures, of all eleven constituent legislatures. (This is now an Alice in Wonderland proposal to some, but I present it as my answer, in the absence of any other proposals.) We have to ask each of the legislatures to send a set of delegates to a conference. The details will have to be worked out — how many, whether they are just legislators or also represent major interest groups, and so on. I think, if the aboriginal people wish to have some of their issues considered at such a conference, then they must be invited to send appropriate representatives, as must the northern territories if they too want their provincehood or their constitutional future dealt with by this conference. The conference will have to take several weeks, if not months, as was the case with the conferences leading to Confederation and in other countries such as the United States and Australia which undertook their constitutional founding in this way.

To arrange such a meeting, one thing we can't get away from is that the first ministers are going to have to meet to agree to such a meeting. They will also have to agree on the rules for the meeting. The first ministers are the only people who can do it. I can't see any other group of authorities in the country in the private sector or public sector who can arrange such a meeting. The threshold problem with the meeting, as any Quebecker here will tell you, is whether the premier of Quebec will even come to a first ministers' meeting to discuss this conference. Moreover, will he come and then agree to go to the conference with Quebec as just one of ten provinces? I don't know. The betting among Quebeckers is that Mr. Bourassa right now wouldn't go. He wouldn't participate.

I prefer that he would, but what I want to stress is that there is a fall-back position. We can still have the convention at this point, without Quebec, providing we see that it will be a two-stage convention.

In stage one, the nine provincial legislatures and Ottawa would get together to discuss constitutional proposals with Quebec absent. That is a clear second choice for me. It would be much better for Quebec to be there, particularly if we are talking about changes in the division of powers and changes in the structure of the federal Parliament. It is much better for the obvious reason that you want to make sure that the nine other provinces and Ottawa don't dig themselves into a position that is utterly incompatible with what might be coming from Quebec. But still, as a second choice to a full conference with Quebec present, there is the fall-back position of a two-stage convention: stage one without Quebec, stage two with Quebec. There will have to be compromises, and one of these would be a two-stage process.

So the constitutional convention will take place in one or two stages. The convention would meet over four or five months — and fairly often behind closed doors by the way, as they did at Philadelphia, and as they did in Sydney and Melbourne, and as our Fathers of Confederation did at Charlottetown and Quebec City, in order to really do some deal-making. But there must be plenty of open televized sessions and there will leaks, *lots* of leaks: we will know enough or think we know enough. After three or four months, the delegates may be able to come out with a set of proposals, acceptable to the delegations from at least seven of the provinces, representing fifty percent of the population. Agreement by all ten would be even better, but there are many changes, particularly in the division of powers and in the federal Parliament, which can be made with just seven provinces. Then if we can get either the seven agreeing or all ten provinces and Ottawa agreeing, the delegations would have to take those proposals back to their legislatures. What one must understand here is that this convention, like the American convention in the 1780s, the Australian convention in the 1890s, and our own in the 1860s, has no final power. A constitutional convention can only draw up the proposals, and negotiate them. Under our Constitution Act of 1982 the proposals would have to be brought back for approval, for ratification, in the provincial legislatures and the federal House of Commons.

Ratification

This is the third stage. About this ratification stage, I would say that if we have accomplished the negotiating stage with a much more democratically representative body of delegates than a first ministers' meeting, a body of delegates that has much more authority with the legislatures they're going back to because they are multipartisan and represent major interest groups, then I think ratification by the legislatures could come fairly quickly. That would be my hope. It would be more or less a rubber-stamp operation.

Now some people argue for a referendum at this stage. But what are the rules of a referendum? We have no referendum provided for in our Constitution Act 1982. We couldn't have just a simple majority decision. Try that in Quebec — that a simple majority of Canadians will decide the future of Quebec! Once you get into designing the rules for a constitutional referendum you are really redesigning the amending formula. That may be worth doing, and one of the proposals coming from the convention might be a new amending formula involving a referendum. I can think of no better way of capping this democratizing of our constitutional politics than finishing it off with a referendum after the changes have been approved by the necessary legislative assemblies. But the rules of that referendum would have to be agreed to by the legislative assemblies of the country.

A Declaration of Independence by Quebec

In my naïvely optimistic frame of mind this is the best scenario I can offer. The other way of dealing with the next constitutional round is through a process outside of the constitutional rules themselves. Frankly I think this is the most likely process. If I were a betting person, I would probably bet on this, although I really don't like it.

The way the next round of constitutional politics might well proceed is through a unilateral declaration of independence by Quebec. This has already been much talked about, particularly by the Parti Québécois and by other Quebeckers. The idea would be that Quebec would just declare its independence of the Canadian Constitution, seek international recognition, and then begin to negotiate with the rest of Canada.

I think the negotiations with the rest of Canada would be on one of two things. It might be for a political or economic association with the rest of Canada. If it is for an economic association, it would also have to be for a political association, because you have to have political institutions to govern the economic aspects of the association. So Quebec might declare its independence, and then turn to Canada and say, now we would like to negotiate an association with you.

The other kind of negotiation is if the declaration of independence has been supported by a majority of Quebeckers who want outright independence and nothing further to do with Canada in any formal sense. Then they have to negotiate to settle some very important separation issues. I just list four of the toughest. The first concerns northern Quebec, the part of Quebec that was added since 1912, and which many argue is not part of Quebec. You only have to raise that question to practically get physically thrown out of Quebec, but it will be raised.

The second is the position of aboriginal people in Quebec. This is particularly relevant in northern Quebec, where they are the majority of people in the part of the province which is most important for its economic future. The aboriginal peoples may not wish to be part of a sovereign Quebec. They already enjoy very important rights under land claims settlements signed by the government in Ottawa and by the Quebec government.

A third issue concerns the rights of the English community, a million or so people who might also believe in the self-determination of peoples, and who might see themselves as having come to Canada not to be part of a Laurentian republic with a clear French majority, but instead to enjoy the rights of Canadian citizens which they still believe are theirs under the Constitution. They might wish to have those rights protected, if necessary by force, against a government which is acting extra-constitutionally. That is not a very pleasant image.

Finally, we have the national debt. How are you going to divide it up?

Now I hope I've said enough about that option at least to make those Canadians who say, "Let them go, let Quebec go" just to slow down for a moment, and to think of the horrendous difficulty negotiating those matters. I agree with Mr. Reuber and others that at the end of the day, after separation has occurred, maybe ten years later, Quebec and the rest of Canada might be no worse off than they were before, and maybe even better off. But what I urge Canadians, both Quebeckers and non-Quebeckers, to think about are the transition costs. These would be dreadful, and the people who will bear them most are the most vulnerable Canadians. They are not myself and my colleagues: we will chatter about it, we'll even make money and sell more books about it. But a lot of vulnerable Canadians will get hurt, and unless you think the gains are really worth it, I hope you will join with me in trying to keep this country together.

Let's not be blasé about separation and negotiating it. It may take a unilateral declaration of independence by Quebec to quick-start a process within the rules of the Constitution Act. It may take that much of a kick in the behind by Quebeckers, playing this game of constitutional chicken, to wake English Canada up enough to start negotiations. It is also possible that we may get into the unilateral declaration of independence simply through frustration in trying to work the rules of the Constitution Act 1982. They may become so frustrating to Quebeckers that they will just give up and make their declaration unilaterally.

My own preference is to begin planning now, right now, a democratic constitutional process, through which all Canadians can gain a constitution which rests clearly on the consent of all the components of this great country. I think that would be a magnificent achievement for our generation.

INTERCHANGE

Question to André Blais:

I know this past summer the youth wing of the Quebec
Liberal Party brought forward a resolution which was
unanimously agreed upon, and this involved not only
transferring powers to Quebec but also having a new
institutional structure which recognized Quebec
sovereignty. How does this square with your predictions
about the commission and the Quebec Liberal Party?

André Blais:

I think it is going to be quite different. As I indicated, in
terms of division of powers, the overall thrust of the
recommendation will be very similar — major transfers
of power to the Quebec government. On the other hand,
I would expect the commission to refrain from suggesting substantial institutional changes. Basically it will
argue for a new decentralized federalism. So I think that
the commission will have a very different view from the
position taken by the young Liberals.

Question to André Blais:

On the Quebec commission, could you say more about
the experts whom the commission is contacting? And if
the aboriginal peoples are going to be so important, why
is there no representative of them on the commission?

André Blais:

The first one is the easiest one so I'll start with that one.
From what I can gather, the commission has basically
decided that "experts" will be persons who are based in
university. All those I have heard about are university

professors. This is the approach they have taken; in my view, again, in order to present an image which is as apolitical as possible. That is basically the rationale behind the choice of the experts.

In terms of there being no aboriginal people in the commission, it seems the calculation behind the decision, which I suppose was a very difficult decision to take, was the assumption that if there were to be representatives from the aboriginal peoples, then the whole focus of the commission might have to shift. With native people involved directly it would be very difficult to focus the whole discussion on the relationship between Quebec and the rest of Canada, which is essentially what the commission and the Liberal government would like to do. So, given that this is their objective, it is in their interest not to have any representatives from the native peoples in the commission. At the same time though they are very important actors, implicitly.

The commissioners will have to consider native peoples' interests as they make their own proposals. My assumption is that the commission itself will not discuss the issue. They will just try to avoid entirely the native issues. I think, though, that it will be a very important implicit consideration, and this will induce the commission, and even more so the Liberal government, to go the federalist route. Going that way could imply that it would be possible not to have a full discussion of native issues since Ottawa would have to be involved later. Québécois are not prepared to discuss these issues at this stage.

Question for Peter Russell:

Are ordinary Canadians going to get involved in designing the Constitution through the hearings process you described? Will this make for productive changes?

Peter Russell:

I am a constitutional conservative. I am happy with the constitution the way it is. But I have a sense of constitutional politics, which I have been studying for a long time in a lot of countries. We should understand two things about it. It deals with symbolic goods, and it generally does involve what we in political science — and this term is often misunderstand — call political elites, rather than the masses. We are going to open it up, but we are not *really* going to open it up. The chattering classes are going to get involved in constitutional politics — the intellectuals, politicians and leaders of opinion groups. And they can get really worked up over symbolic goods and symbolic things, and I think they will want some changes, and they will force some change. I doubt very much whether they will be materially or even spiritually very much better off at the end of the day.

Question to Roger Gibbins:

When the Quebec commission reports and Quebec makes its demands, will English Canada be ready? Even if we undertake federal and provincial hearings, will the federal government be prepared to respond?

Roger Gibbins:

One of the problems of the constitutional process right now is that we have a national government that is impaired for a variety of reasons. I think after the next federal election we are looking at a dog's breakfast of parties, and it is hard to imagine that that will produce any kind of constitutional process or mechanism or leadership that will work particularly well. With respect to the Reform Party itself, my circle of friends — who are wrong more often than they are right — feel the Reform Party will probably capture somewhere in the area of fifty to sixty seats in western Canada. And I suspect that is a conservative prediction.

Peter Russell:

May I add that the kind of Parliament that Roger forecast seems to me to lend itself well to the kind of constitutional political process I am describing, where the key meeting is made up of representatives from all parties in the legislature. Then we get away from this idea that we are going to have only the Trudeau view or, as André Blais was explaining, the Bourassa or the traditional Liberal view presented. There will be a lot of views in there, and I think we are at the point where we have to get partisan politics out of the process somewhat. And the kind of Parliament which Gibbins describes may be almost tailor-made for that, if for nothing else. It may make a mess of just about everything else, but it might be good as a more democratic form of constitutional politics.

Question to Peter Russell:

Mr. Mulroney has set up the Spicer Commission to travel the country and hear the views of Canadians. Don't you think this is just a cynical attempt to regain popularity by a leader who is sitting at 15 percent in the polls?

Peter Russell:

I couldn't care less. I'm more interested in my country.
I don't respect the question. All politicians are always
trying to make themselves more popular. But surely
there is a lot more at stake than whether he is doing
something for a cynical and normal motive. I think
Spicer is well chosen. I think he's got a good grasp on
the communications methods of bringing people together, and of trying to cross boundaries, jurisdictional
boundaries, to get people to interact with one another.
This can work particularly through the electronic media,
maybe in closed sessions rather than big broadcasts with
mass audiences. And that is the process, I think, that is
going to be very important — that people like you
people here have some pretty good encounters, perhaps
through closed-circuit TV with your counterparts at
Laval, for instance. That is the kind of thing that has got
to go on, regardless of Mr. Mulroney's popularity. We
have to engage in that sort of interaction.

Question to André Blais:

You and Professor Cloutier imply that the process in
Quebec is based on the view that in rejecting Meech
Lake, English Canada rejected Quebec. But wasn't the
failure of Meech just a failure of leadership? I think that
English Canadians would have accepted Meech and the
distinct-society clause, but their politicians botched the
process badly. It was a communication problem: they
didn't sell the package properly.

André Blais:

This wasn't the case. It wasn't. I completely agree with
my colleague Édouard Cloutier. It wasn't a problem of
communication at all. I think we have to face the fact

that English Canada rejected Quebec as a distinct society. This is the standard explanation in Quebec, and we've got data to support that. In the 1988 Canadian National Election Study, with which I was involved — and this was before Bill 178 — we asked questions about Meech Lake. There was one neutral question asked which was. "Do you support or oppose Meech Lake?" This was asked without any extra information. In English Canada there was as much support as opposition when the question was put in neutral terms. But we also did an experiment with some of the respondents. When asking the question, we did give extra information that Meech Lake was about Quebec as a distinct society. We reminded people that Meech Lake was about Quebec as a distinct society. When we reminded English Canadians that this was a part of Meech Lake, then twice as many English Canadians rejected Meech Lake as supported it. I think this is a very clear expression that when English Canadians perceived that Meech Lake was about Quebec as a distinct society, then they were against it. When they were not reminded of this, they were mildly positive or divided. And again this was before Bill 178. Let's face it: English Canada rejected Meech Lake because they rejected Quebec as a distinct society.

Question to Peter Russell:

Professor Cloutier has said that the people of Quebec are going to be directly involved in the constitutional process through a referendum. If a new deal can be struck on the Constitution, could there be a national referendum to legitimize it? How would this work?

Peter Russell:

Let me refer to the referendum rules drawn up by the Trudeau government in 1980-81 which, to simplify them a little, required majorities in four regions. But that is something that we'd all have to agree to. One thing that is obviously out is a double majority, (a majority in Quebec and a majority in the rest of Canada). That is something which I don't think would wash. I might point out though that if we could reach agreement on the rules governing constitutional referenda, in my view as a political philosopher, that is about the most profound thing a people could do. We would make ourselves a people, which we've never done. We're not a people; we're some founding peoples, or people who claim to be founding peoples, but we're not yet a people. We're not a self-governing people. We never *made* our constitution in any way.

The most profound sort of social contract we could enter into is to agree on how to govern ourselves constitutionally in a popular way. Who would direct our affairs? Who's sovereign in Canada? That would take a lot of discussion. I hope it wouldn't be ten provincial majorities and one federal majority — that would be the most rigid democratic sovereign. Still, this is crucially important. If we could reach agreement on that, we would have really done something. We Canadians would have accomplished a genuine social contract.

7
IN SUMMATION

Peter Russell

I hope we make it. It is so easy to be negative and cynical, and that view turns out to be right much of the time. But I guess I'm speaking as a patriot. I love my country. I know patriotism is the first refuge of scoundrels, but I don't mind. Canada is a great place, and not for economic reasons. My whole identity is wrapped up in it, and I want to save it. I'll just work at it, and I hope you will too and not take the easy way out unless you want to break it up. And the easy way is to be cynical and smart. I'm not going to be smart or cynical.

Édouard Cloutier

I want to make two points. The first is that this is the end of road. Considering all the process that has begun since 1960, with the founding of the B & B Commission and so forth, we'll see its end product finally within the next two, three, four years at the most. There won't be any coming back to it for a long time. The second thing is that no matter how you look at this, and from whichever point of view you look at this, the word sovereignty comes up in all sorts of ways — talking about Canada, talking about Quebec, talking about the people as the source of sovereignty. So there is going to have to be a definitive settlement of who's the boss; that is, who's the sovereign. This is the basic constitutional question.

André Blais

I would like to point out that there is likely to be very interesting discussions going on within federal parties when the commission in Quebec comes up with its report, and when the Liberal government decides to get on with a referendum. Especially within the Conservative Party, there will be a very tough decision within the Quebec wing of the Conservative Party. A lot of MPs will find it very difficult to decide on which side they stand. Will they vote "yes" or "no"? And there might be very bitter divisions, perhaps resignations, within the ranks of the Conservative Party. We have to consider the possibility that the Conservative government will lose its majority within the confines of the referendum in Quebec. I think this is a very interesting and intriguing question to look into.

Roger Gibbins

I'd just like to pick up on Édouard Cloutier's question about who's the boss. All of us have commented in one way or another about the drift — and indeed the inevitable drift — towards the constitutional sovereignty of the people. I think that is happening. The problem is that we haven't addressed who is going to be sovereign — which people are going to be sovereign? Quebec has already decided that issue, and I think the rest of Canada has accepted it in the Quebec context; the people of Quebec will be sovereign, in terms of establishing their own future inside or outside of Canada. The rest of us, however, those of us who live outside Quebec, have not yet addressed who is sovereign. If it's the people of Canada who are sovereign, then we're on a collision course with Quebec because we have two overlapping sovereign communities. If we decide that it is the people of Canada excluding Quebec, then we have already conceded the game and the game is over. The question is how do we grapple with concepts of popular sovereignty, without having to fragment the community initially to even achieve or mobilize that national sovereignty?

Pierre Fortin

I will make my final point with the statement that economic forces, especially the danger of financial instability in exchange markets and in financial markets in general, will exert a very strong pressure on all parties involved in this round of constitutional discussion to decide, and to decide as quickly as possible. I think that you will see that even if in principle this discussion could go on and on and on until the year 2000, its resolution will be much faster than you might think. I'm not saying that we are going the German way of solving everything within a year, but certainly I don't expect it to last more than a couple of years.

Grant Reuber

We are primarily discussing some form of decentralizing the country. I suspect that the issue goes well beyond Quebec and Canada. The other regions of the country are not as solidified in one block as this discussion might suggest. And I believe that there could be considerable decentralization for the entire country. What we have been talking about is the process for how to do that. That, obviously, is an extraordinarily complicated process, one fraught with all sorts of problems. An important point not to be overlooked, which may make the process less traumatic than otherwise might be expected, is that everybody has an interest in a reasonably orderly process. The economic consequences of having a wildly disorderly process would be very serious for everybody. So there is an economic incentive to restrain the enthusiasms and emotions to some degree and try to find a process. The other virtue of focusing so much on process, in my view, is that it slows things down. I think time is an important element in this. It is not obvious to me that it should proceed quickly.

CONCLUSION

Robert Young

By now most readers will be convinced that Canada is a confederation in crisis. What are the broad options facing us? The first is a general decentralization, with Ottawa ceding more power to all the provinces. The second is some form of asymmetrical federalism, in which Quebec would exercise greater powers or different powers than the other provinces. The third is the constitutional status quo.

From what we know now, this final option would lead directly to a declaration of independence by Quebec. If public opinion in that province continues at its present level of support for sovereignty-association or for outright sovereignty, and if other Canadians refuse substantial reform of the Constitution, then Quebec will opt for independence. It may be true that many Quebeckers don't yet recognize that sovereignty would mean the end of representation in Ottawa, and of equalization payments and Canadian passports, or that Canada would have the upper hand in bilateral negotiations about a host of contentious matters. But it seems equally true that those prepared to play "chicken" with Quebec underestimate the confidence and pride and determination of Québécois. Many on both sides underestimate the costs of separation. Even if the negotiations for disengagement and for joint management of common problems went smoothly, a declaration of independence would impose large transition costs on all Canadians.

A general decentralization might satisfy Quebec demands. But do the citizens of the other provinces want Ottawa to be so reduced in power? In the Atlantic region and in Manitoba, this is certainly not true on economic as well as sentimental grounds. Moreover, a great many Canadians find pride and purpose in Ottawa's nation-building policies — regional development, cultural advancement, universal social programs — and feel a greater need than ever to maintain them in the wake of the Canada-U.S. free trade agreement. They fear that weakening the central government would, as Grant Reuber put it, undermine Canada's "status and potential as a nation." In this view, Quebec nationalism would be satisfied by decentralization (and perhaps only temporarily), but at the cost of Canadian nationhood and collective potential.

Asymmetrical federalism raises the opposition of those who reject any special or distinct status for Quebec. Yet it may offer the only way to defuse the drive towards Quebec sovereignty while preserving the capacity for collective action in the rest of the country. For instance, faced with a list of demands from Quebec such as André Blais predicts, the central government could offer to the provinces power over those areas of jurisdiction which Quebeckers traditionally have felt are essential for their linguistic and cultural survival. Language, culture and communications could be fields of concurrent jurisdiction in which both levels of government could legislate but where provincial law would be paramount. Quebec would probably exercise these powers; other provinces might choose not to do so.

Such a move would undercut one major force, cultural nationalism, which has caused the surge in support for Quebec independence documented by Édouard Cloutier. The economic argument for sovereignty sketched by Pierre Fortin is less well formulated, and it is not so widely accepted among ordinary Quebeckers. At the same time, this move might assuage those English-speaking Canadians whose alienation from Ottawa and resentment of Quebec is discussed by Roger Gibbins. Many of them — including native peoples and recent immigrants — feel that federal bilingual and bicultural policies are demeaning and unfair, and that these policies have been foisted upon them by a central government which is too subservient to Quebec.

This move would eliminate from the constitutional agenda those matters which are most symbolic and inflammatory, both in Quebec and in the rest of Canada. Then, perhaps in a forum like that suggested by Peter Russell, other proposals for jurisdictional and institutional change could be dealt with in the neutral language of efficiency. As in Grant Reuber's paper, the central question will concern the optimal area of jurisdiction for particular government functions, given the current structure of the provincial, national, and international economies. On such issues, there is no reason to expect the Quebec government to be particularly intransigent, though again, it may occupy fields of concurrency which other provinces choose to leave to the central government.

This is one possible route to a solution. There are others. The only certainty is that the constitutional future of Canada is open for discussion. In fact, there must be and there will be a sustained dialogue among the people of this country about their constitution. This should be based on good information and calm reflection. For the discussions to come, the contributions gathered here provide an excellent starting point.

CONTRIBUTORS

André Blais is Professor of Political Science and Associate Fellow in the Centre de recherche et de développement en economique at Université de Montréal. He is also Associate Editor of *Canadian Public Policy*. His research interests include voting behaviour, electoral systems and public policy. He is the author of *A Political Sociology of Public Aid to Industry*, a study for the Macdonald Commission, and is co-editor (with Stéphane Dion) of *The Budget-Maximizing Bureacrat: Appraisal and Evidence*. He has written extensively on Quebec politics, especially on the social bases of Parti Québécois support.

Édouard Cloutier is Professor and Acting Chair of Political Science at Université de Montréal. He took his PhD at the University of Rochester. A specialist in polling and public opinion, he has authored or co-authored several books and many articles in these fields. With the Centre de Recherches sur l'opinion publique (CROP), he wrote *Sondage sur la perception des problèmes constitutionels Québec-Canada par la population du Québec*. Currently he is working on a major study of changes in Quebeckers' opinions about sovereignty.

Pierre Fortin is Professor of Economics at UQAM (Université du Québec à Montreal). He completed bachelor's degree, at Université Laval, a master's at Université de Montreal, and his PhD at the University of California (Berkeley). He taught at Laval from 1976 to 1988, when he moved to UQAM, where he is Director of the Centre de recherches sur les politiques économiques. He has advised firms and business associations and governments about economic and constitutional matters, and is the author of many articles dealing with economic fluctuations and stabilization policy, and with labour markets.

Roger Gibbins received his BA Honours from UBC (1969), and his MA (1970) and PhD (1974) from Stanford. He was appointed to the University of Calgary in 1973, and is currently Professor and Head of the Department of Political Science. He has pursued a variety of research interests spanning western alienation, Canadian constitutional politics, political belief systems, Senate reform, American and Australian politics, and Aboriginal politics. He has authored (or edited) nine books and many refereed articles and book chapters. His publications include *Prairie Politics and Society* (1980), *Regionalism: Territorial Politics in Canada and the United States* (1982), *Conflict and Unity: An Introduction to Canadian Political Life* (1985, 1990), and *New Elites in Old States* (with Neil Nevitte, 1990).

Grant Reuber studied at University of Western Ontario and Cambridge, and took his PhD at Harvard. He has worked with the Bank of Canada, the OECD, and the Ontario Economic Council, and served as Deputy Minister of Finance in 1979-80. He was Senior Economist with the Bank of Montreal, and was President and Chief Operating Officer of the Bank from 1983-87. At the University of Western Ontario, he taught in the Economics Department from 1957 until 1969, before becoming Dean of Social Science and Vice-President (Academic). He is the author, co-author or editor of several books and monographs on Canadian economic policy, and also has written many scholarly articles and press commentaries.

Currently he sits on the boards of major companies, research institutes, and artistic organizations.

Peter Russell is Professor of Political Science at the University of Toronto, where he teaches Constitutional and Judicial Politics. He has written many articles on these topics, and is author, co-author or editor of *Nationalism in Canada*, *Leading Constitutional Decisions*, and *The Judiciary in Canada*, among other books. As well as serving as an advisor to government he has been President of the Canadian Law and Society Association (1987-89) and is currently President of the Canadian Political Science Association.

Ronald Wintrobe is co-director of the Political Economy Research Group at the University of Western Ontario, where he is a member of the Economics department. A leading Canadian scholar in Public Choice, he is co-author of *The Logic of Bureaucratic Conduct*. He has written many articles on bureaucratic competition, party systems, altruism, and dictatorship. Currently he is working on a major study of the logic of dictatorial regimes.

Robert Young is co-director of the Political Economy Research Group at the University of Western Ontario, where he is a member of the department of Political Science. He has written widely on Canadian politics, as author or co-author of articles and monographs on industrial and trade policy, federalism, bureaucratic politics, Maritimes politics and regional policy. He is working on a study of industrial development policy in Ontario.

SUGGESTIONS FOR FURTHER READING

Banting, Keith and Simeon, Richard, eds., *And No One Cheered: Federalism, Democracy and the Constitution Act* (Toronto: Methuen, 1983).

Beck, Stanley M. and Bernier, Ivan, eds., *Canada and the New Constitution: the Unfinished Agenda* (Montreal: Institute for Research on Public Policy, 1983).

Beckton, Clare F. and MacKay, A. Wayne, eds., *Recurring Issues in Canadian Federalism*, Royal Commission on the Economic Union and Development Prospects for Canada [hereafter Macdonald Commission], Research Study No. 57 (Toronto: University of Toronto Press, 1986).

Behiels, Michael, D., ed., *The Meech Lake Primer: Conflicting Views of the 1987 Constitutional Accord* (Ottawa: University of Ottawa Press, 1989).

Brodie, Janine, *The Political Economy of Canadian Regionalism* (Toronto: HBJ-Holt College Publishers, 1990).

Cairns, Alan C., *Constitution, Government and Society in Canada: Selected Essays* (Toronto: McClelland and Stewart, 1988).

Cairns, Alan C. and Williams, Cynthia, eds., *Constitutionalism, Citizenship and Society in Canada*, Macdonald Commission, Research Study No. 33 (Toronto: University of Toronto Press, 1985).

Canada, Federal-Provincial Relations Office, *Amending the Constitution of Canada: A Discussion Paper* (Ottawa: Minister of Supply and Services Canada, 1990).

Canadian Public Policy, Special Issue on the Meech Lake Accord, XIV: supplement, September 1988.

Cohen, Andrew, *A Deal Undone: The Making and Breaking of the Meech Lake Accord* (Vancouver: Douglas & McIntyre, 1990).

Courchene, Thomas J., *Economic Management and the Division of Powers*, Macdonald Commission, Research Study No. 67 (Toronto: University of Toronto Press, 1986).

Dufour, Christian, *A Canadian Challenge/Le défi québécois* (Halifax: Institute for Research on Public Policy, 1990).

McRoberts, Kenneth, *Quebec: Social Change and Political Crisis*, 3rd ed. (Toronto: McClelland and Stewart, 1988).

Milne, David, *Tug of War: Ottawa and the Provinces Under Trudeau and Mulroney* (Toronto: James Lorimer & Company, 1986).

Milne, David, *The Canadian Constitution: from Patriation to Meech Lake*, rev. ed. (Toronto: James Lorimer & Company, 1989).

Olling, R.D., and Westmacott, M.W., *Perspectives on Canadian Federalism* (Scarborough: Prentice-Hall, 1988).

Russell, Peter H., Knopff, Rainer, and Morton, Ted, *Federalism and the Charter: Leading Constitutional Decisions — A New Edition* (Ottawa: Carleton University Press, 1989).

Shugarman, David P. and Whitaker, Reg, *Federalism and Political Community* (Peterborough: broadview press, 1990).

Simeon, Richard, ed., *Intergovernmental Relations*, Macdonald Commission, Research Study No. 63 (Toronto: University of Toronto Press, 1985).

Simeon, Richard and Robinson, Ian, *State, Society, and the Development of Canadian Federalism*, Macdonald Commission, Research Study No. 71 (Toronto: University of Toronto Press, 1990).

Smith, David, Courtney, John, and MacKinnon, Peter, eds., *After Meech Lake: Lessons for the Future* (Saskatoon: 5th House Publishers, forthcoming 1991).

Watts, Ronald L. and Brown, Douglas M., *Canada: the State of the Federation 1990* (Kingston: Queen's University, Institute of Intergovernmental Relations, 1990).